Casey at the Bat

Casey

The Story
of My Life in Baseball
as told to *Harry T. Paxton*

Random House ✕ *New York*

at the Bat

Casey at the Bat

1

When I was a ballplayer in the National League, a manager told me, "There's one good thing about having you around. This is too dead a ball club. I'd rather have somebody like you with a little life—somebody that does things that are a little out of the way."

Well, I guess I've been doing things that were a little out of the way for most of my life in baseball. It gave some people the idea that I was just a comedian. When I was signed to manage the New York Yankees after the 1948 season, many of the writers couldn't understand why I was brought in to handle such a big job. They had watched some of my work, evidently, as a manager at Brooklyn in the thirties, and at Boston later on. They thought that I wasn't very serious, and that I never cared very much about winning games, and that I was too easy to get along with, and so forth.

But half the time I was too serious, maybe, with my work. When I don't win, I'm good and mad there at night. But if you think you're going to do better just by being serious all the time, and never telling any stories or doing any kidding around—why, you're a little mistaken. Some people never could understand that.

At the time the Yankee job came up I was managing at Oakland in the Pacific Coast League. We had just won the pennant out there. Edna, who is Mrs. Stengel, enjoyed the Coast League very much, and she thought possibly I wasn't going back to the big leagues. And there was a question in my mind, too. There were half a dozen times before then that I was going to quit baseball altogether. I'd been a ballplayer and a manager for thirty-eight years. I'd worked at numerous places. I didn't care much whether I went back up.

Of course, I'm glad I did go with the Yankees. We started off by winning five straight pennants, which was a record, and five straight World Series, which naturally was also a record. By the end of my twelve years there we'd won ten pennants and seven world championships, which I guess is as much success as a manager ever had over that span.

But I'm just as proud of some of the jobs I held with clubs that were never in the first division. I was allowed to manage anywhere from three to six years for ball clubs that should actually, if they thought it was the manager's fault, have fired me in one year. Fifth place was as high as I ever finished at Brooklyn, and at Boston it was also fifth. So I must have satisfied the business manager, or I couldn't have held the positions that long, the way they change managers in baseball.

If you look it up, you find that the average manager holds his job less than three years. There were sixty-one changes of big-league managers in just the last ten years. I have very great sympathy for men who didn't get the opportunity they should have at managing because of lack of ability in the players, or maybe in the business office financially. Very seldom do people get to manage as long as I did.

Different men have been credited with getting me picked for the Yankee job. When I was discharged in October 1960, I didn't see anyone taking credit for that. I'll give you the truth. What the owners of that ball club, Mr. Topping and Mr. Webb, really wanted was for all of us to get fired after the 1959 season, when we finished a bad third in the American League.

They became panicky and worried. They said, "This man has blown"—that's the manager. "Maybe the coaching has blown"—that's two. "Maybe the players have blown"—that's three. "Maybe the team spirit has blown" —that's four.

If they'd discharged me then, they'd have had a good grievance. And any fan would have said that something had to be done about that Yankee machine—"The old guy's age has got him."

But my contract had another year to run, and they didn't try to fire me in '59. And the club hadn't blown, as was proved in 1960. The Yankees came back and took the pennant by eight games. They won their last fifteen games of the regular season, and they won three games against a red-hot club in the World Series. And we were all right up to the seventh inning of the last World Series game.

Later on I'll tell you more about how I came to get hired, and then fired. Anyway, I'm not mad at those two owners. You work at a place for years and years, and finally new men come in and old ones go out. The owners think the new ones are better and they get rid of the others. The ownership has the right to do that.

Wherever I've been, as long as someone was paying my

salary, I've tried to give a dollar and twenty-five cents in work for every dollar paid me. In other words, I might not win, but the effort would be there, whether I was at the ball park or away from it. What else would I do with my time? I don't play golf. I don't go to picture houses. So I put the time in trying to plan things that would help the ball club.

I had to work very hard when I was a ballplayer, too. Some men play good without putting effort into it. Others have to go jump around. I used to have to work as hard as everything—wiggle my shoulders and my body and my arms—to be able to do well.

I was an outfielder in the National League for almost thirteen years. I was very erratic. Some days I was amazing; some days I wasn't. I'd have a good year, and then not so good a year. I wasn't what you'd call a consistent player except in a number of big games. I was a star in World Series games and in important games with clubs that won pennants.

But I found out that if you're an erratic player like I was, and you're trying hard, you're very seldom booed. People don't notice that you're doing bad as long as the effort is there. They always thought I was all right as long as I wasn't being a comedian.

One of the biggest mistakes I ever made was at Brooklyn in 1917. I'd been a holdout over the winter. The owner, Mr. Ebbets, wanted to cut my pay something like $1700, even though I'd hit .364 in the World Series the year before. I finally had to take about a $1300 cut.

I didn't like that. So when we came to Ebbets Field to start the season, I took one of the contracts they'd sent me, took a pair of scissors, and started down to right field during practice. People yelled to me, "Did you get your money back, Casey? What kind of contract did you get?"

And I held up the contract and cut a piece off it with the scissors to make it shorter. "I didn't get such a big one," I said.

Well, in the Brooklyn office they didn't think that was so smart. They said, "He's getting too fresh and he don't use enough tact."

And to tell you the truth, I didn't have a very good year that season. Now if you're being a comedian, the minute you don't do well, then they've got you. Because that could be a case that I wasn't trying. And I wasn't that kind of a player. I told you, I had to try hard every day.

The Brooklyn club dropped to seventh place that year from winning the pennant the year before. After the season Mr. Ebbets said it was terrible, and he told me, "We owe for this ball park too, and you haven't helped me pay for it." And I said, "I must have given you a concrete pier for it when I took that pay cut."

So I was too fresh for them, and it ended up I was traded right over to Pittsburgh the next year.

I was always too aggressive. I made too much trouble the first few years I was in baseball. I got started that way when I was in sports at Central High School in Kansas City, Missouri. In basketball games somebody would grab my trousers in the back and hold me, and I'd get rough. And when we started a student football team, that's when we got into most of our trouble. Because we'd sometimes play not a recognized school, but an independent team. And those games became too rough. You went over to Kansas City, Kansas, and you ended up smashing each other too much.

In professional baseball the first time I had real trouble

was with Aurora, Illinois, in my second year. This was 1911. We were playing in Rockford, and there was this umpire whose name was Arundel. I used to kick a lot on balls and strikes—argue and argue and argue—and he kept telling me I shouldn't argue that long.

So he called me out twice this day, and I was getting good and mad. And the next time he called me out he commenced laughing and rolling his shoulders. He went, "Ha, ha, ha, ha! You're a big shot! Ha, ha, ha!"

While he was laughing at me I was walking back to the bench, which was more than a hundred feet away from home plate. Finally he turned around to get ready for the next hitter. I sneaked back on my toes still carrying my bat, and when he bent over the catcher I unloaded on him with the bat. I really got a good drive off him. I was put out, naturally, and the game was forfeited.

When the umpire sent in his report, the league president, Charley Morrall, decided he was going to fine me. It was lucky for me this was before baseball had its first commissioner, Judge Landis, or it would have been worse.

But I needed the money to go to dental college, which I was doing in the off season at that time. I'd already bought two suits of clothes and a straw hat. So after I got back to Aurora, I saw the business manager and said, "Everybody's sick at our house. I have to have money to pay up our bills, and I have to go to dental college. Can you advance me some money for my tuition?" And thank heavens, he did.

Another time I went too far in a ball game was in the 1923 World Series. I was playing for John McGraw's New York Giants against the Yankees. I wasn't supposed to be one of the stars, but I won the first game with an inside-the-park home run in the ninth inning.

From then on, Babe Ruth and the boys gave me a good going over. They promised me, "Watch out now when you come up there to bat. You're going down." They were going to brush me, and you know what a good brushing is.

Well, in the third game I hit another home run that won the game. It was in the seventh inning, and the ball went into the right-field bleachers. As I was circling the bases I made like a bee or a fly had got on the end of my nose and was bothering me. I kept rubbing it with my thumb, and sticking my five fingers in the direction of the Yankee bench.

I heard about that in a hurry from Commissioner Landis. Baseball had been put on a higher plane by Landis, and he didn't like that kind of an exhibition, with 60,000 or more people from all over the United States sitting in the stands and watching. The American League people had been complaining, and Landis told me, "If you ever do that again, I'll promise you one thing, you won't receive a dollar of your World Series share." So that was a good example for me, and after that you can bet your life I always remembered I was in a ball park with outside people watching me.

I don't mean I never was in any trouble on a ball field again. Managing at Toledo a few years later, I got in a couple of fights and the league suspended me a total of twenty-six days. I had to watch my team from the stands. And my owners said, "Look, now, what's the use of having you hired as a manager? We'd rather have you become the manager and stay the manager and let somebody else sit in the grandstand."

Out at Oakland, just before I came to the Yankees, we used to get in fights with the San Francisco club, because the rivalry there on the Coast League was so great. It was like Brooklyn and the Giants used to be in New York. A free-for-all would break out during a game, and our tough players would run out on the field, and their tough players. It would look pretty good, so I'd run out to get into it too.

I was in my late fifties then. And every time you looked at a picture of the fight afterward, you'd see maybe fifteen or eighteen men standing up and fighting with each other, but you couldn't see me. There'd be a long arrow pointing down at the ground at the bottom of everything, and there'd be a line on it that said, "Stengel." So I found out that I was slipping.

Jimmy Dykes was managing the Hollywood team in the Coast League then, and he said to me, "Don't you think you're getting a little old to be doing all that fighting?" And I commenced thinking, "Well, he's probably right." So after that I decided to become a bench manager and let the players do the fighting.

Everybody brings up fights, and asks me about fights, and wants to talk to me about fights. I have been in some trouble that way. But when I came into baseball the rule was that you took care of yourself on the field against the other team or your own.

At the time I started in the big leagues with Brooklyn in 1912, some players wouldn't let you take batting practice if they could help it. So I had some cards printed. And when I'd go over to the batting cage and a man would say, "Who are you?"—although I might have been with the club two months—I'd reach down in my pocket and hand him a card that said, "I am Charles Dillon (Dutch) (Casey) Stengel. Would you please allow me to go up and hit in batting practice?"

Dutch Stengel was what they called me back in Kansas City. In one of the neighborhoods I lived in as a boy there was this rich family by the name of Marsh. Their boy would ask the kids over to kick a football in his big yard. He didn't know my name at first, and he called me "Dutch." So I became Dutch in that neighborhood, and it followed me all through school.

In baseball I went by the nickname of Casey. It was partly because I came from Kansas City, and people would call me by the initials of my home town—"K.C.," which turned into Casey. I think another reason the name stuck was because of the poem, "Casey at the Bat," which DeWolf Hopper was reciting on the stage all over the country.

It wasn't until years later that I actually met DeWolf Hopper. I was with the Giants, and I won a game from Cincinnati with a home run off Adolfo Luque, a great Cuban pitcher I very seldom could hit. McGraw called me over to the dressing room after the game, and I thought he might be going to give me a little bonus or something. But he had this visitor with him, and he said, "I want you to meet DeWolf Hopper. You've heard him recite 'Casey at the Bat.' "

Anyway, in the poem, Casey, naturally, made a big strikeout. Well, I was built very strong when I was a young ballplayer, and I'd swing too hard and miss the ball, and they'd say, "Strikeout Casey."

When I came home after my first time in the big leagues in 1912, I was offered fifteen dollars to play in an exhibition game against Walter Johnson, the greatest pitcher in the American League. I'd hit .316 in seventeen games in the National League—they hadn't found my weaknesses yet—and I thought I was one of the best players in the country. And I said, "It isn't the fifteen dollars. I want to hit against Walter Johnson."

Johnson came from Coffeyville, Kansas. They were having a homecoming celebration for him, and this exhibition game was part of it. They rounded up two teams of professional players. Earl Hamilton, who was with the St. Louis Browns, pitched for our team.

Well, the first time up I swung at Johnson's pitches, and I struck out. Three times he threw a ball up there that I had swings on; I missed them. The next time I said, "I won't swing so hard at this man. I'll just meet the ball." So I didn't swing as hard. I still missed the three. I hadn't even fouled a baseball.

The third time up I said, "I'll bunt." So I went to bunt, and I couldn't even touch the ball with the bat. That was nine strikes and I hadn't fouled a ball.

Finally, the fourth time up I hit a long foul off him down the left-field line. That's the only ball I touched. The next two strikes he threw past me.

We lost the game, 1-0, and one of the Kansas City papers the next day said it was "due mainly to the inability of Stengel to hit in the pinches." That was a funny one, as I'll explain. A fellow named Kilduff, who batted ahead of me, got two hits off Johnson. He was about the only man on our team to get on base all day. And naturally I failed to drive him around.

Johnson had twenty strikeouts that day—Earl Hamilton had nineteen—so I wasn't the only man that was missing the ball. But afterward people would say to me, "So you're that great man they were talking about in 'Casey at the Bat.'"

2

People who didn't get to know me until after I was in baseball don't always believe this, but I was pretty shy and quiet as a youth. I remember that at the basketball games in high school you could bring your girl. And she would get to wear a white sweater—the Marilyn Monroe type, you know—and when you'd come in with her, everybody would go, "Woo-oo-oo-oo-oo!" And that bothered me. I got so that I never wanted to take a girl to the basketball game. I used to say I had to leave early to get ready to play, because if she came down with me, then I'd have to take her home.

Today it doesn't shock me to stand up and talk before one thousand, two thousand, three thousand people. I don't try to talk about their business. I tell them about baseball, because baseball should be my subject. But in school I never would do any speaking, except one time in my third year when the basketball players were asked to talk to the students in the study hall and get them to cheer harder when we were behind. Miss Morey was the teacher, and when she called on me I was game, with just forty or fifty people in the room, where I wouldn't stand up before the whole school in the assembly hall.

I remember when we won the state championship with the baseball team, I was asked to accept the trophy in assembly, and I couldn't do it. I gagged.

The principal's name was Cammack. He called me in his office the next day. "Dutch," he said to me, "I'm so surprised. It hurt me a little that you couldn't get up and receive that award for the school."

I never did enjoy school too much. The first one I went to was the Woodland grade school. They called them ward schools in Kansas City at that time. My teacher was Mrs. Kennedy. She had an idea that you should be a right-handed writer, even if you were naturally left-handed, which I was. Whether you thought with the left or right side of your brain, you had to write right-handed.

We sat two at a desk in that school, and when we practiced penmanship, if everybody wrote right-handed, why, we were all in gear. But if somebody did it left-handed—well, I guess you've noticed when you're sitting down at a table eating, it gets confusing if somebody next to you is left-handed and you're right-handed. You're nudging each other with your elbows. And it was that way with our penmanship exercises.

I noticed later on in baseball that you always remembered what the tough managers told you. Like John McGraw. He was strict. He would fine you. Well, the same thing goes when I think back on my schoolteachers. I remember if I didn't do my penmanship correctly—if she caught me switching over to my left hand—Mrs. Kennedy would keep me after noon hour. She'd put me in a closet and close it up and say, "Well, you stay here for half an hour."

She broke me of it, and I write right-handed to this

day. But I'll have to admit I'm not too good as a writer.
I get mixed up on that writing. I don't know whether that
helped to start me on Stengelese or not. It's a very shocking thing to me, this Stengelese—which is what they call
the way I sometimes become careless in my speech.

I picked up in my penmanship after the first four or
five years. But it gave me no inspiration to write. Today,
while I can write a fair hand, I still go up on one side and
down on the other, and my letters aren't even or vertical.

But then I know so many people right now—intellectual
men, men that can dictate a letter amazing, and be outstanding people to stand up and give you a line of conversation and wonderful English. And yet when they sign
their name you can't read it, if they don't have the name
printed on top of the letter or underneath. And every
time they sign their name in a restaurant, people come
up and argue with them. And you can't blame the head
waiter, because the man is signing for the tab, and you
can't tell who it is. It looks like chicken feet.

Anyway, I don't blame Mrs. Kennedy for making me
change over in my writing. She was just following the
rules in the Kansas City schools at that time. And when
I got into baseball I thought it was a great thing that she
made me write right-handed. I became a good fielder—
after being an awkward kid—because I could use my
right hand better. I stayed left-handed in throwing and
hitting, but I had to use my right hand, naturally, in
catching the ball. And because of my penmanship, I was
more agile with my right hand than any person who had
stayed left-handed in everything. I was almost ambidex-
trous.

That helped me more as a ballplayer than the writing
ever would. And as a manager, I never cared whether

somebody else thought I was stupid as long as I was doing the job. In sports, the thoughts are a little different.

For instance, I don't like to have a catcher looking over at me all the time from home plate to get me to call the next pitch for him. So I found one on the Yankees, Yogi Berra, that I didn't have to do it with. The people when I went there wouldn't believe it, that Berra was going to get to call the signs. There were numerous people that said, "This guy can't think enough to call signs." Highly educated pitchers told me that. But Mr. Berra has got a sports mind. And he did a beautiful job for me for many years.

And that's the way with the manager. If he knows what to do in sports, he is very good. Like Leo Durocher. And here's something about Durocher that he may not know himself. If I'd taken one of the opportunities to run another club that were offered to me right after the Yankees discharged me, there were two men I'd have tried to hire as assistant managers. One was Durocher—he hadn't been signed by the Dodgers then. The other was Ted Williams. Mr. Williams and I are friendly. He seems to have my methods of play. He knows everything about hitting. And he might become a great manager.

Getting back to Durocher, I can see why he's been a pretty good manager. He'll take a shot. Lefty O'Doul, who used to manage against me in the Coast League—he'll take a shot. I don't think either of them could show you any degrees from the large universities. Of course, I've seen managers that had the degrees, and were very good and brilliant at managing too. I'm just saying that in baseball it's a different thing.

A big thing in my managing that seemed to confuse a lot of educated people was my platoon system. When we were having that bad year in New York in 1959, one of my owners remarked—and it got back to me—that he couldn't understand why I did so much platooning. And here I'd been winning with it all those other years.

I've never really explained my platoon system, which I'm going to do further on in this story. But without telling too much about it right now, my platoon thinking started with the way McGraw handled me in my last years as a ballplayer on the Giants. He had me in and out of the line-up, and he used me all around the outfield. He put me in when and where he thought I could do him the most good. And after I got into managing I platooned whenever I had the chance, long before I came to the Yankees.

Or maybe it goes back even further. I platooned myself as a boy in Kansas City. I'd look over a team and pick out the weakest spot so I could win a position. I became a third baseman left-handed in high school because of the inability of the third baseman. He wore big magnifying glasses, and I said, "I know I can beat him out."

The next year they had a good third baseman, so I became a second baseman left-handed. Why? Because it looked like there was an opening on the club there. The third year I was a pitcher. Why? Because it looked like they needed a pitcher.

I started in professional baseball as a pitcher, and when I couldn't make that, I switched to being an outfielder. So I know something about what it means for a ballplayer to be platooned around in different positions.

Anyway, the platoon idea began to bother some of the people my last few years on the Yankees. Another thing the office worried about was whether some of the players were running around too late at night. The club is supposed to have had detectives following different players at times. I don't know whether they did or not. But I can tell you that wasn't what got the pennant back for the Yankees in 1960. It was the players' ability, and the fact that their interest was to win the pennant.

There are men that don't have bad habits, but have bad spirit. I'd rather have men with some ability and some fight and some spunk, and who like their teammates. Some of the players who got bad publicity were men I could never have won without over that number of years.

These are pretty well-known ballplayers. You get big money when you play baseball if you are a Mantle. Mantle should get money. Mantle excites the public. Mantle has been booed in New York. I don't know why it is. It's silly for them to boo him. He still fights to win and wants to stay in New York City.

Billy Martin was a good, winning ballplayer for me in Oakland, and he was when I had him in New York. I couldn't have done without Martin on some of the plays he made. Somebody else couldn't have made them.

Maybe there's better pitchers than Whitey Ford. I couldn't have gone without Ford. What would I have done in the 1960 World Series if I hadn't had Mr. Ford around? He pitched two games and never allowed them to get any runs, and if I'd been nimble enough to start him sooner, he'd have gone in and pitched the last game and maybe offset things.

Now every club has rules that there's a time to come in. There is no manager that ever lived that would say, "Stay out as long as you want to." And I know I've never said it would pay anyone to run around and stay out after hours.

Players violated the nights on Mr. Stengel once in a

while. But the four that did, or five, or different men in different years—they had the spirit of that ball club, and were trying to win, trying to get to home plate.

We don't advocate drinking. But to say that a ballplayer doesn't ever take a drink—regardless of advertisements, some do. Now no ballplayer should ever get into the habit where he drinks before a ball game when you have night ball. Those kind of men never played for me over two years. When I had one of those boys, I said, "Well, this man is limited. We should get what we can out of him, and then if he doesn't want to change—why, disappear him."

But if you're in a pennant race you can put up with any kind of character except a man that is lazy. A lazy man is a terrible thing on a ball club. And he may be a man that never breaks a rule. He says, "I go to bed at eleven o'clock every night." But he's not awake when he's on the ball field.

In other words, he doesn't get interested in baseball. He says, "Oh, the same old thing over and over. I wish I was in another business." Well, there you have a bad man.

In my day a man who was very poor generally wanted to become a ballplayer if he could. You started out in baseball with salaries from $75 to $150 a month. That was a very good salary in those days for a kid. If you could make that kind of money in professional ball, you could bring some of it home and help your parents. It was very seldom that you found people who could afford to have their kids not work but go to college.

With me the idea at first was that I was using the baseball to go to dental college. My father told me that if I was going to play baseball all summer, I couldn't hang around a poolroom all winter and be a bum. I had to do something in the off season. So I had to put away enough money during my first two years in baseball to go to dental college in the fall.

If I hadn't made the big leagues fairly soon I probably would have become a dentist. Or if I'd dropped back to the minor leagues in my first five or six years, I would probably have been a dentist.

But I stayed on in baseball for fifty years. I played with the dead ball and the lively ball, and I saw men manage with the dead ball and the lively ball. And I managed with the lively ball myself.

3

When I was a boy in Kansas City my brother Grant Stengel was the one everybody thought would be a professional ballplayer. He used to carry me in baseball. From the time he was fourteen and I was twelve he could play with all the fellows up to eighteen years of age. My father would make him take me along, and they'd put me in the outfield or wherever anybody wouldn't show up.

He was very clever at baseball. Now in those days we didn't play by all the rules, and as we went along, my brother and I worked up a trick play. He would play shortstop and I would pitch, and he used to take a potato with him. We'd get one as near round as we could, and he'd slip it in his back pocket or in his waist above his belt. And when there was a runner on second base and they threw down there to try to catch the runner off, Grant would catch the ball and try to tag the man. Then instead of throwing the baseball back to me on the mound, he'd throw the potato. And the runner would go to take a lead off the base, and my brother would tag him with the ball.

We pulled that one day when we were playing a game on the Parade, which is still there in Kansas City— it is on the way to the baseball park. We lived about twenty-five blocks from there at the time, and that trick started a free-for-all fight. When they started after us, everybody on that playground, we found we couldn't win. We had to run all the way home.

So we cut that potato trick out. We didn't try that any more on the other team's grounds.

Grant got me on some of the leading independent teams that were in town. He would always be the best player they had. Then one day we made a trip in a surrey to play a game in Dobson, which was a suburb. On the way back guys commenced hitting and wrestling with each other, and Grant slipped off the surrey. His foot got caught in the brake and he sawed off part of his heel. He never got well for six months, and it made his one leg smaller than the other as far as circumference was concerned. That caused him to give up the idea of becoming a ballplayer.

He no doubt would have advanced to the big leagues if it hadn't been for that accident. When I went into professional baseball myself, there were a lot of people in Kansas City that remembered what a tremendous player my brother was, and for the first three or four years they thought he was the Stengel who was playing ball. They'd meet me in the off season and say, "I see your brother is doing good. He's in the big leagues." And I'd have to say, "That's not my brother. I'm the one that's playing ball."

Grant had five or six strong points in baseball, where I was more of a work horse and had to fight my way and play awful hard during a ball game to be good. He was skinny—he used to claim it was because I got most of the food at home—and he wasn't a slugger. But he could hit and place the ball and very seldom struck out. He could run like a deer. He was a good fielder, an accurate thrower, and he was very sharp and bright on the bases—a good slider. My brother was what was wanted in base-ball at that time, before the change from the dead ball to the lively ball.

They say you can build up any subject and then tear it down. And I could build up the methods they used to play by in baseball and show you that half of them aren't worth a quarter today, because the conditions of the game are so different. And what's required of the ballplayers is different.

They go for the loft hitter now. The batter tries to hit a long fly with men on third and second and the infield in. In olden times, with a dead ball, he wouldn't be such a great hitter, because he'd just be hitting high flies. When I started in the big leagues the pitcher would pitch to make them hit a ball in the outfield. He didn't worry about the home run, with the best sluggers hitting only fifteen or twenty a year. He'd look back at me, a green out-fielder, and give me a little sign to go right or go to the left, and he'd make them loft a high pitch.

But now the outfield is a dangerous place to have them hit, with the lively ball and with the parks in many places being smaller, because of the extra seats that have been built in. The ball caroms off the modern concrete walls much sharper than it used to off the old wooden fences. Or it goes in the stands, and the best outfielder just can't get up in the grandstand and catch that home run for you.

In the old days a big thing was to hold a runner on second so you could throw him out at the plate on a single. The pitcher would hold him on, hold him on, hold him on, and the outfielders would play short so they could get the ball to the catcher quicker. And the catcher with that heavy equipment would block off the plate, and the runner would hit him. So most all the fights that started in baseball then were at home plate. There was a collision all the time.

You couldn't be an outfielder if you didn't have a good throwing arm. If you were big and hit hard but were slow-footed and awkward, they tried to make you a catcher, or they tried to have you be a first baseman. They couldn't afford to play you in the outfield.

But in Ruth's era they commenced saying, "Get the big fellow if you want to win." Today the base-running is still important—first to third on a single, first to home on a double—and the pitcher still tries to hold them on. But with the lively ball the outfielders have to play so deep that they generally can't throw a man out anyhow. So some heavy hitters play the outfield now that don't throw so well.

A player had to be able to do more different things in the old days. A small man who couldn't hit the ball very hard was all right if he could execute the various plays. We used to use a heavy bat and choke up on it. You weren't supposed to strike out often. They'd try and get you to be a good runner on the bases, and be slick at the plate. You had to sacrifice, hit and run, hit behind the runner, and do all those things. The object was to get a man on, get him to second, and then get him to third and home.

Now they'd say, "Why are you trying to play that kind of a game? You're going to finish fourth instead of first."

And you possibly will, with those big hitters on the other teams coming up and murdering you. The big men at the present time, they go for home runs. Of course, they outsmart themselves many a time, when they've left three men on and two men on. They fail with men on third and second. They're afraid to just meet the ball, and they often strike out.

Then why is it the pitchers seldom go nine innings any more? Some people think the pitchers used to be in better shape, but I don't think they were. A pitcher in the wintertime—there generally wasn't any gymnasium for him to work in. In the summertime they didn't run the pitchers between games as much as they do now to keep them in shape.

But the old pitcher was throwing the dead ball, and he used to be able to cheat more. The ball was darker. The infielders would spit tobacco juice or licorice on it. A new ball would come into the game, and it was passed around the infield—the man on third would give it a whack, the man on short would give it a whack, the second baseman would give it a whack. And when you got it back again you'd say, "Where's that new ball?" You had a black ball. That was done with licorice and tobacco juice, and with black dirt on the infield.

Then some of the old pitchers threw the spitball, and some would throw the shine ball, where they'd keep paraffin alongside their trouser leg and shine one side of the ball with it to make it break sharper. If the ball had a tear in it in just one spot, that was what the pitcher wanted.

Today the balls are slicker. They use seventy balls in a game. The umpires examine the ball all the time, and if there's a scuff mark on it, they throw it out. They try to keep you from throwing spitters, or doing anything to make it easier to sink the ball.

The old pitchers who went the nine innings learned to pace themselves. They could stand out there and use that arm and use rhythm—a curve ball and a fast ball and a change-up. Those were the three main pitches they had in those days. They pitched half with their arm and half with their head.

Nowadays you can't wait on the pitcher to pace himself. That lively ball with the cork center and the yarn wrapped tighter—there's so much slugging that the pitcher has to bear down all the time.

So why aren't the batting averages big like they used to be? Well, one reason, which I mentioned, is that everybody tries too hard to slug the ball. And then we have ten pitchers to shoot at you, instead of four like years ago. A pitcher goes out there and puts something on every pitch, and he goes as far as he can, and then you take him out and put somebody else in.

A great thing with a lot of the present-day pitchers is the slider. They can't make a living, some of them, without it. Every hitter now wants to use the light bat that's got a little handle. So these pitchers put the slider in on the handle, or they try to pitch away and put it on the bad part of the bat. And the slider can be a great pitch, but it's hard on the elbow. I think that's why more pitchers get crippled arms now.

But they have to try something, because it's dangerous to pitch today if you haven't got a lot of stuff. I'm surprised at some of the pitchers that stay in the game. They should quit baseball, because they're really getting shot at by those hitters, and it's a risky business.

Now let's look at the gloves the players use. In my youth

they never used to have fancy gloves for men. You wore a glove for protection, not looks. So that's what you did in baseball. You had a pad for your hand. In those days nobody knew enough to build a large pad. Baseball gloves used to be made very small. They just went around your hand. You had to use your hand with ability and skill. You had to catch two-handed to hold the ball.

Today they've got traps in the gloves. The gloves are beautiful—some five fingers, some six fingers. They put a piece of leather between the thumb and the front finger. What happens the minute they catch the ball there? The glove closes like a trap. So half of them catch the ball one-handed. They do at first base—they fold the glove sideways. It becomes like a jai alai game.

They used to have bumpy infields, and the outfields were bumpier than the infields. Now the grounds are kept better. At Yankee Stadium they have an outfield like a pool table. It's level. This was done because of the fact that Mantle stumbled out there in the 1951 World Series and turned his knee. Since that time they have spent large sums of money to make the outfield smooth.

So the outfielder there can run in and charge a ground ball like an infielder. It won't bounce bad. And he can run and catch a fly ball. In the olden days you'd have to run over bumps and holes in the outfield. You couldn't charge grounders. You had to get down on one knee to protect the ball from going through.

The infielders got more bad hops. Managers used to tell them to play the bounder. In other words, when the ball was hit, the infielder would sometimes back up to get it on a higher hop. Nowadays they don't back up. They go toward the ball, because many of the hitters are so fast sprinting down the line to first.

But even with the better equipment and the better grounds, you have to have more ability to be an infielder or an outfielder today, because the lively ball comes at you quicker. You have to start faster because of the speed of the ball. It goes through the infield faster. And if you're an outfielder—in my day we could run and overtake the ball if the park was large enough. Now you can't get to it half the time. You can't overtake it unless you're a Mantle or a DiMaggio or one or two other amazing men that get such a start it's noticeable that they're really catching up with that ball.

That's why I say the outfielders of today are greater. And the infielders are greater.

There used to be more base-stealing, of course. One reason they eventually cut out a lot of it was that most men, when they tried to steal bases, would get thrown out half the time. Then you've wasted half your hits. A base stealer is a valuable man for the club only when he makes it almost every time—the way Max Carey used to for Pittsburgh and the way Aparicio does for the White Sox today.

They also used to bunt more. You had to learn to bunt in those days, and it was easier with the dead ball. But you can't bunt a lively ball as good, and every infielder runs in at you. The odds generally are against bunting now. So you don't have many good bunters. But you have better long-ball hitters. The hits and drives are terrific.

The players are maybe traveling poorer today, in spite of the airplanes and everything, because they have to play at night and then sometimes the next day in the afternoon. They have no set hours for eating and sleeping, whereas we did, because we only played in the afternoon.

But when we got hurt—we didn't have anything like

the training rooms they have now. Once when I was playing for Brooklyn, I ran into Charlie Grimm at first base,
and I thought I'd ruined my back. I commenced gasping—
I couldn't get my breath. So Wilbert Robinson, the manager, said, "Ah, you ain't gonna hit that spitball pitcher
anyway. You might as well go in the clubhouse and let the
trainer work on you."

Well, this trainer was in a hurry to get back and watch
the game, and he didn't think I was really hurt anyway.
So he got me on the rubbing table and just took a bottle
of Sloan's Liniment—the kind they used on horses—and
poured some in the palm of his hand. He slapped that on
the base of my spine and went right up my spine with both
fists. And within five minutes I rose right off the table,
because that stuff was burning me to death. I couldn't
play for nearly a week after that treatment.

So in some ways baseball is better now. But as far as
the players are concerned—if a man was a good hitter
with the dead ball, why couldn't he hit the lively ball?
And if he was a good fielder with a little glove, why
couldn't he be a good fielder with a trap glove? And
the pitchers who were good then—why couldn't they ad-
just to the livelier ball and the harder hitting of today?

So some of the players I see now, they certainly could
have played in the old days. And there were plenty I saw
in olden times that could have played today.

4

✂ There were a lot of things boys could do in Kansas City around the turn of the century that didn't cost very much. One of them was baseball. Most everyone went in for baseball because it was a cheap sport.

The bats were cheap—you could get one for fifty cents in a drug store. Or you'd try to get hold of an old wagon tongue and whittle a bat out of that, because it would last forever. It was made of the strongest wood you could get, which was hickory. And today nobody wants it— they want a light wood, like ash.

The gloves also were inexpensive then. To think that now you have to pay $18 to $39—it's a severe thing today for a man to give a boy a baseball glove. And the balls used to be cheap. Of course, we'd never have a ball over three days but what it was an old baseball. It would start tearing, and you'd have to get some black adhesive tape and tape around it. But we kept it going that way.

And there was always ground to play on. The big cities in the East were built right up against each other, with apartment houses or row houses all in a line. Most kids there had nowhere to play except out in the streets, which kept the ballplayers in the East from developing very fast.

But in the smaller cities in the West there was open space. The houses weren't all built together. Some of them had immense yards. There were many open lots. It was nothing unusual to play in lots where people kept cows, because there weren't the dairies then that there are today.

When you played baseball in a lot, you just had a path to first, a path to second, a path to third, a path to home. And the rest of it was not a lawn, it was grass that grew up or died, and that would be your infield. Then in the outfield, you'd just have a field where you ran in and caught the ball. But you *did* get to play.

Shinny was another cheap game we had. You'd pound up a tin can, and then hit it with sticks. It was a little like the game called hurling that I noticed was played in Ireland when I made a visit there in later years.

Then we had roller-skating. Anywhere we wanted to go, we used to go on roller skates. We never had ball-bearing skates in those days. So we used to take grease from the underground cables that pulled the cable cars, and put it on our skates to make them go faster.

If it wasn't roller-skating, it was bicycling. My father gave me a tandem bike for Christmas when I was about ten. That became a fighting vehicle. It caused more fights around our home and the school than anything we ever had. Nobody wanted to ride in the second seat. Everybody wanted to be the number one man.

My brother and I used to collect pigeons and train them to go out at certain hours of the day. And if we ever did anything wrong, it was that we would try to steal other people's pigeons. We would put out feed for them. Others would do the same. One month we would have his pigeons, and the next month he would have our pigeons.

At one time I had a dog we called Sport. We were living on Park Street then, and I was attending the Garfield ward school. This was a tremendous dog. I had him trained so he could climb a tree on a ladder. The big problem was to get him to come down. He naturally couldn't turn around, and to back him down that ladder was tough. I sometimes had to get him around his body and go down the tree with him myself.

I could lie on my back and this dog would climb up on me and do several tricks. If my brother and I were hungry, we'd take Sport to another neighborhood and have him perform. The people would come out of their houses to see him, and they would be there with their kids, and we would have him do all these tricks. And afterward we would tell them we were hungry and out of our own neighborhood. We'd get a sandwich or two and give old Sport a bite of it. He was our meal ticket.

In the wintertime we had sledding. If you got a little sled for Christmas, that was your big gift. There were no automobiles on the streets to bother you—just some horses and buggies and wagons. We used to have long snowslides off every hill that wasn't too populated. We would get everybody in the neighborhood and make up a long sled train, and see how far we could go from the top to the bottom with a good start.

Another famous sport was snowballing. When wagons would drive by, we'd watch for those elderly teamsters that had clay pipes. It was great if you could knock that pipe out of his mouth.

We'd be fifteen or twenty of us. We'd go to one of the big homes on Independence Avenue, where they had those large front yards. We'd make big walls of snow, and then put our snowballs behind them. And when the teamsters came along, we'd let fly about fifty snowballs at one time.

If we hit them good, they'd stop that horse and that big wagon, and they would chase after us. We would always be some distance away, and boy, we started pretty good. But once in a while there'd be one that would catch us and beat up on one or two of us.

I used to belong to the St. Mark's Episcopal Church. I'd get twenty-five cents or fifty cents for turning the pump of the organ. They also had the Brotherhood of St. Andrews, and I joined that. The director was Mr. McKinnon. He had a son by the name of John that played on my Central High baseball team at one time. Well, after Wednesday night meeting Mr. McKinnon would walk out with a high silk hat on, and we'd snowball him. That high silk hat—why, that was a dandy.

That church group followed up until we moved out of the neighborhood and I dropped some of the church work, which naturally nobody is proud of. I still hear from my Sunday school teacher. She says we were pretty bad kids at times. And I thought we were doing a fine job in that church.

At night in Kansas City they used to have a curfew whistle they blew at nine o'clock to get kids off the street. You'd see us kids running like anything to get home at night, because the police picked you up if they caught you out after nine o'clock. I can remember one policeman, Harry Arthur, and I never will forget his name, like those schoolteachers that had little love for you.

One thing we liked to see was the little wagon from the confectionery store that would deliver ice-cream freezers to people who were giving parties. If we saw that wagon, somebody would trail after it on a bicycle and find out where it went. Then we'd go there at night, and while everybody was inside singing and dancing and entertaining, we'd grab this ice-cream freezer off the back porch and take off with it.

One night we tried that at the preacher's home. This policeman, Harry Arthur, was following us and he caught us. He got the ice-cream freezer back and took all our names and then chased us home. The next day at school they announced that they wanted four of us to call at the preacher's home and apologize. And our parents and everybody thought it was terrible, because two or three of the parents had been inside the house at the party that night.

We never thought much about whether we were rich or poor when we were growing up. Each neighborhood we advanced to—we moved about seven or eight times—we'd get acquainted with people. There would be poor people who didn't have anything, others who had a little more, and others who had everything anyone ever wanted, with horses and coachmen and so on and so forth.

There were the Dickeys, and the Nelsons who owned the Kansas City *Star* and *Times*. There were the Kempers, the Ridgeways, the Perrys, the Marshes.

But we kids all played together. The best thing I ever had, I guess, was that the family allowed everybody to come to our home. My mother always used to like everybody in the neighborhood, and they could all come over and use our back yard and the front yard. Therefore we'd get to play in a rich man's front yard too.

I've never paid too much attention to who my ancestors were, but a lady in Rock Island, Illinois, who is a cousin of mine, sent me the whole family tree a while ago.

I found out that my Grandfather Stengel came over to this country from Germany with his family in 1851, at which time he was about thirteen. They lived in Utica, New York, at first, and then settled in Rock Island in 1855. Four years later he got married to Katherine Kniphals, and in 1860 my father was born. His name was Louis E. Stengel.

I never got to see my Grandfather Stengel. He died of TB when my father was only four. Three years afterward my Grandmother Stengel got remarried to a man named Charles Wolff, that I did get to know later on.

On my mother's side the names were Jordan and Dillon. Her mother was the sister of Judge John F. Dillon, who was on the Iowa Supreme Court and then on the United States Circuit Court, and was counsel for the Union Pacific Railroad. Her father was John B. Jordan. They named her Jennie Jordan. She was born in 1861, a year after my father.

The Jordans lived in Davenport, Iowa, which is just across the Mississippi River from Rock Island. So my mother and father eventually met. The were married in 1886, and went to live in Kansas City, Missouri. On family trips later, to see my father's side of the house in Rock Island, we'd also see my mother's people in Davenport.

My step-grandfather was a gunsmith in Rock Island. His shop was right down at the wharf, where a man by the name of Lobson had a ferryboat that used to go between Rock Island and Davenport. They didn't have a bridge then.

When I was only about five years old my father had me make a visit to my grandmother in Rock Island. And they would put me to work in the gun shop at noon hour while my step-grandfather was eating his lunch. He would have me look after the shop, and if I sold a gun I would get five or ten cents commission.

One day a man came in and said, "I want a rubber-barreled shotgun." I never stopped to think that there wasn't such a thing. So I went and pulled back every showcase in the place. He kept saying, "I don't like that gun. Get me a rubber-barreled one."

Finally he started laughing and said, "Don't you know who I am? I'm your Uncle Will Jordan from Davenport. Judge Dillon is here from St. Louis and he wants to see you."

Each year around Christmas my step-grandfather would send my brother and me a gun. It would be an air rifle, naturally—not a twenty-two or anything of that sort. Then he started to send us pistols, but there would just be a wad in it and powder.

Once I was trying to get the wad out. And I broke open the gun with my hand still over the end of the barrel, and the trigger snapped and drove that wad right into the palm of my hand. Well, I didn't want anyone to know what I'd done. I kept trying to go along without saying anything about that wad in my hand. But after five days my hand swelled about double, so I couldn't keep it a secret any more. My mother got very excited, but the doctor just took my finger and pulled back on it, and that wad popped right out.

Another thing they say happened to me—I don't recall much about it myself—was when I was on a family visit to Rock Island at the age of four. My brother Grant was pulling me along the trolley tracks in a little wagon, and there was this deep hole full of water. Well, he must have got too close to it, because I went into the hole, and if a man hadn't come along and pulled me out I'd have been a goner. My sister Louise says that's the first time I got my name in the papers. A Rock Island paper had a story about how "little Charles Stengel was saved from drowning."

I had another close call like that when I was older. A crowd of us went to a swimming place near a Milwaukee Railroad bridge outside Kansas City. Everybody dove in, so I dove in too. And the water was over my head, and I couldn't swim. Fortunately there was a fellow in the group that was a very good swimmer. He dove in and saved me for a lot of good times and trouble.

One very early thing I remember is a visit to my mother's people in Davenport. My mother had me wearing long curls like a girl at that time. Well, my Grandfather Jordan was retired. I'd follow him around, and I'd copy what he did. He chewed tobacco, so I'd make like I was chewing tobacco too.

I told him, "I'd like to get a hair cut like you." So he gave me fifteen cents and I went out and got my hair cut. When I came back, and my mother and my grandmother and aunt saw me, they took and grabbed me and slapped me for getting those curls cut off. They said, "Who told you you could get your hair cut?" And I said, "My grandfather." Then they sure did jump on him.

They went down to the barber shop and collected all those curls off the floor they could find. They kept them for years in an envelope back home. But I was tickled to death to get them cut off, because it made me look like a man and they'd had me looking like a little girl.

I was the baby of the family. The oldest is my sister Louise Stengel. She was born late in 1886. I remember she was a good student in school. She still lives in Kansas City.

Then came my brother Grant late in 1887. He's a widower now, and retired. He's making his home in Prairie Village, Kansas.

Charles Dillon Stengel was born on July 30, 1890. That's myself. A lot of people say I'm older than that, and there's a few that think I'm younger. But that's the right date, and I have the birth certificate to show for it.

The first home that I lived in was on Agnes Avenue— 1229 Agnes. It's still there. It was a very small home, and with me being the third child in the family, my father naturally began to look for another place.

About the only thing I can recollect about Agnes Avenue, up to the time I was five years old, was that we used to play games about Jesse James and his gang. Their careers were over, but they were still the most noted crooks at that time. There was Jesse James and his brother Frank, and there was also Coleman Younger. They had been Missouri men, and we boys thought they were something. They used to ride in with five or ten men and hold up trains and rob banks, and so on and so forth. They weren't considered to be like the crooks are at the present time. They were supposed to be very honorable. They wouldn't shoot you if they didn't have to. They'd just show their big guns and grab the money and run.

I took after my father in looks. He was built strong, something like myself, and he had large ears, which I do. He was an agent for the Joseph Stiebel Insurance Company in Kansas City. They also owned a street-sprinkling company, and they told him, "If you stay here, you can get out of this insurance business in three or four years, and we will give you the sprinkling business."

So he went into that. This was before the city did the street-sprinkling. My father had this water wagon. It was a wooden water tank, only they put wheels on it and horses pulled it. You pushed a pedal with your foot and squirted water on the street. My dad would collect from where he sprinkled, and anybody that didn't sign up, he would naturally leave the street dry in front of their place. He sprinkled for the merchants on Grand Avenue and the other main streets, and he also had fifteen or twenty of the blocks where the wealthy homes were.

He used to play cards with some of the merchants, and when he'd win they'd say, "Well, how could anybody beat a man that can make money selling something as cheap as water?"

That sprinkling business only lasted about eight or ten years after my father got it. When the automobiles commenced coming into Kansas City, with those slick rubber tires—they didn't have any tread on them like they do today—they would slip and slide on the hills that had been sprinkled. So complaints would go in to the city. And it got to where less people wanted the sprinkling downtown. The city finally came in with modern apparatus and took over the job, and my father's business was what you'd call defunct.

That was around 1915 or 1916, and after that he was more or less retired. By then I'd got to where I could help my family out from my salary as a big-league ballplayer.

My father always took a great interest in my ballplaying. When I hit my first World Series home run in New York in 1923 he was standing outside the Kansas City *Star* building, where they had a big board that showed how the game was going. They got the information by telegraph and put it up there.

Well, they tell me that the minute the news came about my home run, my father turned around and started running all over the town. He ran to call on everybody that had ever paid for sprinkling, and he said, "Did you hear what my boy Charlie did?" They called me Charlie at home. "My boy Charlie hit a home run!"

I think that helped him come back from a heart attack he'd had not long before—going around like that and telling all his friends and the people he'd done business with about my home run. And he lived on for many a year to come.

5

My father liked to see my brother and me playing baseball. When his business got poor, he'd follow us to games every Saturday and Sunday. He thought my brother was the best player, which he was, but he wanted me to play too. My father thought it was fine for me, except one time when he heard me use profanity. Then he said I'd picked it up from the other kids.

My dad had grown up around Rock Island, where he hunted and fished, and that's what he loved to do. He was a great man for meat and fish. Most every dollar he made he used to turn into food. He'd go to the best market downtown, and in the wintertime he did like to get good steaks. And he certainly did like fish, if it was local fish—they didn't have the refrigeration to ship fish very far in those days.

We used to put out the best meals in the neighborhood, at least we thought so. Everybody likes the way mother cooks. And that's just the way it was at our house, everything that my mother cooked—the potatoes with the gravy, and I could see that gravy running around. Nowadays a lot of people say, "Don't touch the gravy." And I'm over seventy, and I've been taking gravy all my life. I used to take that big gravy spoon and put it in those mashed potatoes. And I'd flap them down on the plate, and then get a good steak and put it on top of that.

My mother was great on making preserves. And she'd make things like catsup, and put up all kinds of food in jars. She also was great on lemon pie. She could buy two lemons and make them go a long way. We'd have lemon pie maybe once a month—in those days it was pretty hard to get lemons out in the middle part of the United States.

My brother never could get fat. He'd eat and eat and eat, but he stayed skinny. As I told you, he always claimed that he was robbed and that I got most of the food. Well, I will have to say that my mother was very easy on me. I was the youngest, and she possibly did favor me a little.

There were chores my brother and myself had to do at home. We would have to wash the dishes, and then we sometimes had a cow to look after. My father loved to have a Jersey cow and have that milk. My brother and I were supposed to milk it. And I wasn't such a good milker, but Grant could milk like everything. He could strip that cow down good. So I'd take a big switch and keep the flies off while he milked, and then I'd deliver milk to some neighbors who bought it.

My father used to give us a little tip money if we got extra milk out of that cow. So to get more tips, we took to adding a little rain water to the milk from a cistern we had in the back yard. My father would come home and see those two big crocks of milk and say, "My, isn't it wonderful how those boys handle that cow?"

But we commenced using too much of that water, and a neighbor made a complaint. He said, "We don't know whether we want your milk any more. It looks too thin."

My father said, "Why, my goodness, I can't believe that.

This milk is from a fine Jersey cow, good old Fawn. We are feeding her bran . . ." and so on and so forth. Then finally he found out that we were putting water in there, and he sure did give us a going-over.

When I was in grade school my father used to keep buff Cochin chickens. And then he got interested in cockfighting. He went out and bought about four or five roosters at different farms around Missouri and brought them home. This was at 510 Park. And my brother and I were supposed just to irritate these fighting cocks a little— keep them mad and keep them separated.

My father would take them out to where this cock pit was, out toward Independence, Missouri. They must have won two or three times. And finally he got what looked like a champion.

Grant and I said to each other, "I bet he can whip anything around here. We can't go to see those cockfights, so let's put him in with our own chickens."

We got in that barn, and we'd just put this champion rooster in there when my mother called us for lunch. And when we came back out after lunch—we have now lost which rooster? The champion rooster. Those buff Cochins really took after him.

And I want to tell you something, you should have seen my father when he came in that night and found his champion rooster was dead. Grant told my father we didn't know anything about it. Grant said the door to the cage must have broken open, then the rooster got out and jumped into the coop where the other chickens were. That was a height of about fifteen to eighteen feet this rooster was supposed to have flown over. My father wouldn't quite believe all that, but as I remember he never did find out the truth.

As a boy I was supposed to be fairly good on fighting because I was so strong. I was large for my age—I was very large around the chest. If I could get a hold of a fellow I could wrestle him and get him down where I could hit him pretty good.

I found one fellow who was a little too tough for me. We had trouble with this group after a ball game at Exhibition Park, and this fellow said, "I'd like to fight you at any time." Well, I didn't care too much about fighting him, but after the fellows in our neighborhood got through talking to me, I thought I could whip him.

So they took me over to see him and we started in. He had taken up boxing and he wouldn't let me get in to grab a hold of him. He'd slip one way and then the other, and he kept hitting me with his left and knocking me back. And I said, "This fellow hits harder than anybody I ever saw." That was one fight I didn't win.

The next day in school they told me that he had had a big metal nut in his pocket, and whenever I got in to wrestle with him, he'd screw it over his finger and take a pop at me. He'd hit me right over the temple. And for five days after that, every time I'd go to open my mouth my whole scalp would move. So I told the kids that next time they could find somebody else to do their fighting.

Anybody that was real fast, I had trouble with. Like my brother. He was lighter than me, even though he was older, but he could run as fast as anything.

One time when I was in high school I wanted to go and see this girl. Her name was Margolis. She lived about five blocks from where we were living then on Brooklyn Avenue, and she said, "Yes, come over and meet my mother and father."

I had to have some equipment to go out with, and I had

no regular salary coming in—we were running out of cash money. When I went up to dress and looked in the closet, I said, "Darn it, my shoes always run over at the heels. I'll just put on my brother's shoes"—nice-looking patent-leather shoes that he had sitting in the closet.

My brother had such a small foot I wasn't sure I could wear his shoes. I pulled on them and pulled on them and couldn't get them on. Finally I grabbed a hold of the tongue, and I pulled so hard I tore the tongue off. So then I took some black adhesive tape that we had in the cellar and taped the tongue on.

Well, when I got over to the girl's home this night, I was sitting with her, she was introducing me to everybody, and these tight shoes were really giving me pain. I looked down, and that tongue had slipped off. So I had to sit and put my toes over my ankle where the tongue was. And I couldn't sit still because my feet were cramping me because of the pain.

I had to make a hurried exit from the young lady's house. I forgot her good looks. And the family were very glad I was a wonderful boy and didn't stay too long.

After I got home I patched the tongue back on again and hid the shoes in the closet. A few days later my brother yelled, "Mom, Mom, has Charlie been wearing my shoes?"

She said, "No, I don't think that boy could wear those shoes with those big feet of his. How could he put them on?"

I was in the kitchen. I never said anything, but sure enough, Grant came down and commenced raving. He said, "I know you wore them! You tore that tongue off of it!"

I got up with him, and he had a very good way with

me. He took a crack at me in the argument, and then he started moving. And when he'd move I couldn't catch him, because I couldn't perambulate as fast as he could with my legs and my arms.

Another time I took a box of candy that he'd brought home and hidden in a dresser drawer. I knew he was going to take it to his girl, but I was seeing a girl myself. So I happened to pick that box up, and I kind of cut it open and unwrapped it, and took it over to my girl friend. I said, "We'd better eat it all." And we ate until we were almost sick.

I took the empty box back home. I got a brick and pounded it into about fifteen squares. I put it in the box, with some cotton around it so it wouldn't rattle, and wrapped the box up again and put it back in the drawer.

And then my brother took it over to his girl's. And he opened the box, and there were those bricks pounded up. So I got another good popping when he came home.

My brother actually had a great disposition. He always got along with everybody. Grant never had any ideas on high finance. He would love to make a hundred dollars a month, and if he made the hundred he could live on the hundred. He just didn't care about anything too much except to live according to the conditions of the time.

He had very good habits. Whenever he gambled, he was a ten-cent gambler. He never let it get into the dollar side. He'd start shooting dice with fifty cents, and after three and a half hours he'd still have ten cents. He was what we called "Ten Cent Grant."

First he worked for a feed store, then later he worked for my father, driving the street-sprinkling wagon. My father wanted him to go into outside business, but Grant thought driving that wagon was the greatest job in the world. He enjoyed working with the horses, and he enjoyed scaring everbody that was a friend. They'd be walking along the street with their heads down, and he'd give a hard squirt over the curbstone and up on the sidewalk, and wet the shoes and trouser legs of the men or the bottom of the girls' dresses. And that tickled him to death.

I used to like to ride along on the wagon with him. We'd say, "There comes somebody up there about a block." We'd drive along, and all of a sudden we'd give him that long squirt. So everyone that went to school with us knew what our father's business was, and who was the one who was very big on the sprinkling wagon. My brother— he sure could manipulate that. He used to get everybody so mad. He was a real expert with that foot.

And he used to have the horses trained pretty good. He'd get the horses to chase him and line up and do anything he wanted. They got to be almost like circus horses. He had them so well trained he could move that wagon around and squirt that water anywhere he wanted to.

My father told me, "If I hadn't put that boy on the water wagon he'd have gone through high school and college." But Grant would rather make his money where it was fun with the work. He could have had a terrific job with a Buick agency, but he didn't take it. He finally ended up in the taxi business. But several years ago he came down with TB and was in the hospital a long time, since when he's been in retirement.

As a kid I did different kinds of work myself. Sometimes I'd get paid for doing something special around the house, like carrying in a ton of coal or wood. I carried that coal in buckets instead of wheelbarrows. I'd put a bucket over each elbow, and two in my hands, so I could carry four buckets at once. And I'd get twenty-five or fifty cents for it.

That was one way my brother and myself could get money for things like ice cream sundaes and candy. Another thing we liked to do was see the vaudeville shows in Kansas City. We would go whenever we had the extra money. We'd go downtown to Keith's Theater—the Orpheum—on Saturday afternoon. It was several miles from our house, so we'd hop rides on the cable cars. They only had one man operating them. He had to collect the fares and also run the car. We'd jump on in front while he was in the back of the car, and then when he got up to the front we'd hop off. That would take us three or four blocks on our way. And then we'd do the same thing on the next car that came along.

On Saturday afternoons at the Orpheum schoolkids could get to sit in the gallery for ten or fifteen cents. My brother and I sure did enjoy that vaudeville. Some people have said that I had ambitions to go on the stage myself. That isn't true. I never had any idea of doing that.

There were times when we needed every extra quarter we could earn to help out at home. I could always get a job as a water boy. Just think—I could make three dollars a week carrying buckets of water around to the men on a construction job. And I thought that was a very good way of strengthening my arms.

Another job was with the Alpha Flower Company. This was after school hours and during vacations. I'd deliver flowers to the rich people who ordered them for a wedding or a big party. If it was out of town, there was a bicycle for me to make deliveries. I worked for that company about a year and a half, and I think I did a fairly good job, because they hired me back a second year. Often they're sick of you by that time.

One summer I worked for the W. F. Grant Company, which put out an epileptic medicine. First you had to wash the bottles and make sure they didn't leak, then you'd fill a bottle with medicine just so far from the top. Then you'd take a cork and drive it in just far enough. Next you put glue on one side of the bottle and put a label on. Then you put the bottle in a case. And when you made up five cases, your day's work was over. I got so I could be out of there in two hours.

In the meantime I was beginning to find out that I could also occasionally make a little money playing baseball for different teams. I liked that better than anything.

6

The team I've spent the most time with in baseball, naturally, is the New York Yankees. Next to them it was the Brooklyn Dodgers. The Dodgers were the first big-league club I played for, and later on they were the first big-league club I managed.

When I played at Brooklyn, one of the infielders was a man I'd gone to grammar school with back in Kansas City. He was Ivy Olson. I entered the Woodland School at the age of six, and as I went along I found out that the big bully there was Ivy Olson. He was five years older than I was, and he was tough.

In the big leagues he also was tough. He played third base and then shortstop at Brooklyn. He was an arm tagger. Some men, like Dave Bancroft, were hand taggers. They'd tag you so quick you couldn't hardly tell whether they'd touched you or not. But Olson dove right at the bag and let you hit the side of his arm. He let you come to him, and as you came in he would raise his arm.

If a man came with his spikes high, Ivy would say, "The next time you come in like that, I'll put this ball down your throat." That's the way they used to try to scare you from coming in and spiking them at second base. Or they'd say, "If you slide into me and knock me away it's all right, but the minute you cut me you're keeping me from drawing a living. If you cut me and handicap me, watch out, because one of us is going to get you."

Olson was a little rough at tagging. If you were a tough fellow, he'd tag you toward the face. One day he tagged Jim Thorpe pretty rough. Thorpe was playing with the Giants. He had won a lot of medals at the 1912 Olympics, which they later took away from him on the grounds that he was a professional.

Well, Thorpe was supposed to be the strongest man in the world. He got mad at Olson, and in the argument Olson never let Thorpe get within five feet of him. Ivy always said, "Never let a man get closer than five feet, or he may hit you first." And if Ivy did have to fight, the other man never did get to hit him first.

Olson was not the greatest third baseman or shortstop I ever saw, but he was one of the brightest. He very seldom pulled bonehead plays. He was a tremendous man at catching runners off bases, and he loved to get two men on the same base. He would get them so mixed up that he could tag them both out.

He was just fair as a batter, but he studied and improved on that too. He was what they called a first-ball hitter, only he was really a first-strike hitter. He wouldn't take pitches for strikes. He'd take a bust at everything that was over the plate.

As a baserunner he never believed much in sliding into catchers when they blocked home plate. He'd say, "Why slide into him with his shin guards on and break your leg?" So he'd run into them standing up. He figured that if he bumped them hard enough they couldn't catch the ball.

He was good at baseball when he was at the Woodland

School, but what I remember best is another game we played. At recess and noon hour we used to line up in two teams against a wooden fence, and each team would try to push the other down along that fence. It wasn't a tug of war with a rope. This was pushing instead of pulling.

Ivy Olson was the captain of one of the teams, and if it wasn't going good, he'd pick up an extra boy that was standing around and say, "Get in there and take this man's place." And if it was you he was replacing, you wouldn't say, "I am not getting out," because he pulled you out and shook you, too. He was the strongest fellow in the school, and naturally they let him be the boss. Because he was the boss.

I've talked before about my teacher at Woodland, Mrs. Kennedy, who made me write with my right hand instead of my left hand. The principal of the school, Mrs. Buchanan, was just as strict. If you did anything wrong, she would call you in and use a switch on you. She had a switch with a little nick in it, and she would give you two or three belts on your leg with the switch. If it broke she would take a little rubber hose she had there and give you a couple of good whacks.

If any parents complained that she was too rough, she said, "Well, I had to do that because the switch broke." And I noticed that she always had bad switches.

Whether Mrs. Buchanan and Mrs. Kennedy were great teachers or not, they used to make you measure up. If your parents wouldn't do it, they would. Parents couldn't go down much and alibi for their kids. And I didn't see any of those kids getting into serious trouble in later years.

In my studies, my trouble with writing slowed me up in every subject. We had to write our homework by hand;

and in class, we had to write the answers to the questions up on the blackboard, or else we had to write them out on a piece of paper at our desk.

Now anything you can't do well and don't enjoy, you generally fall behind in. I think another reason I didn't keep up with my age group in school was the fact that we moved so much. During one move my family held me out of school for a term. Then when I switched to the Garfield School at the age of thirteen, they seemed to think their school was brighter, and they set me back another half year.

I finished up at Garfield on January 27, 1906, when I was fifteen. At the graduation exercises they made me sing "School Days." I was a terrible singer, and when I got up, the fellows made like they were going to walk out. They let on like they had to go to the men's room. And that disturbed me so much that I had to stop singing. But they made me finish it. That was the last job I've ever done in the singing line.

Two days after leaving Garfield I started in at Central High School. I wasn't very strong at studies there, either. I never belonged to any of those classes in English literature and the rest of it, where they recited from those Shakespearean plays. I knew enough not to get in it.

A bunch of us would be going down the hall between classes, and when we passed those fellows in the Shakespearean class, we'd say, "Ye gods, men! And how are you today?"

A big man at that Shakespeare was William Powell, who became a famous movie actor in later years. He started in Central two years after I did. He could get up and recite, and he was a terrific actor in school plays. I remember him wearing Italian uniforms and all. And he'd dress like a woman, and he could do it. He also used to play basket-ball—he cracked one of my teeth with those sharp elbows of his.

One of my English teachers in the high school was Mr. A. F. Smith. When you wrote a theme he'd mark the mistakes with blue, or maybe with red. And he'd read themes aloud in class, and if he read mine, every sentence would be blue, blue, blue or red, red, red. And everybody would say, "That must be Dutch's theme."

Mr. Smith was very enthusiastic about sports. I was playing on the different teams, and I noticed he quit reading my themes to the class. He knew if he failed me, I would be out of sports. He was a serious man and a wonderful teacher, and he followed my career for years after I went into baseball.

I was active in sports outside the high school as well as in it. My brother Grant got me on the Armour baseball team, which was a packing company's team. Then there was the Northeast Merchants. I wasn't as good a player as the rest of them, but my brother would get me on there half the time.

In football I was better than my brother was. He liked the game, but being pretty light, he didn't care about tackling anybody head-on. He would rather be an end and tackle from the side as somebody went by, instead of taking that contact. He wasn't too much for that football business. He was mainly a baseball man.

Getting back to baseball, the first money I ever made was with the Parisian Cloak Company team. That was a very large store owned by Siggy Harzfeld. Fred Deichmann was the manager of the team. I played with them most of the time I was in high school, and finally I thought I ought to commence receiving some money. So I asked for three dollars to pitch a game for them. They wanted to give me a dollar-fifty, but I held out for three dollars and finally got it.

The baseball also came in handy during the summer of 1907, when I was in my second year of high school. A bunch of us went out to try to earn some money in the Kansas wheat fields at harvest time. Herschel Ressler was one of the fellows. We got all the way to Pratt, Kansas, more than two hundred miles from Kansas City. A farmer out there hired us, but the work soon ran out and so did our money. The sheriff in Pratt found us sleeping in the park. He got us fed and started us back home.

On the way we passed through a place called Council Grove. Three of us were Central High baseball players, and somebody recognized us and asked us to play for Council Grove in a game they were having with Redington. We helped them win—I drove in the deciding run in the eleventh inning. So we got some food and lodging out of that, and made it the rest of the way home to Kansas City.

We used to travel any way we could. Once some of us took a train to Lawrence, Kansas, to see a track meet. When the conductor came to collect our tickets we ducked past him and ran several cars away. Then we hid ourselves by getting into a group of fellows shooting dice.

Or we'd bum rides on top of the cars. I did that one time, and the cinders from the engine were getting in my eyes, so I decided to lower myself down between two coaches. I lost my hold and dropped all the way down. It was lucky for me that the train was moving very slowly—it was going to stop for a crossing. I was able to give myself a last push out of the way before any cars rolled over me.

My last two summers in high school—1908 and 1909—

I rode the trains as a regular passenger. I was with a traveling semipro team called the Kansas City Red Sox. We would go twenty-five or fifty or seventy-five miles every day. We went as far one year as Ogden, Utah, and the next year, Cheyenne, Wyoming. And on the way back, if we couldn't draw any more in baseball, we'd book basketball games, as some of us were experienced at that.

Several of the players on that Red Sox team went into professional baseball. One great player was Claude Hendrix, a pitcher. He went up with the Pittsburgh club in 1911 and pitched in the National League ten years. He was a twenty-game winner three different times.

We had a man by the name of Gibson that went as far as the American Association, and a pitcher named Hal Rustahaven that looked like he was going to be great. He had a trial with the Giants, but didn't make it. Another good player on the Red Sox and at Central High was Bill Gardner. He didn't play professional ball.

In the country hotels we stayed at we'd sometimes play jokes on each other, like putting a piece of rubber hose in a man's bed to make him think it was a snake. One night there were five or six of us in a room, and Hal Rustahaven was out late. We set a bucket of water on top of the door. It came down on him when he walked in. He was going to whip us all, but he finally calmed down.

Rustahaven lives in Blackwell, Oklahoma, now. He sometimes makes winter visits to Southern California, and he's dropped in a couple of times to see me at home in Glendale.

That Red Sox team was organized by Ira Bidwell. He was the most amazing promoter I ever saw. He was just a kid in Central High, and an athlete on the teams there. He'd send out letters during the winter while he was in school and get a traveling schedule all arranged for the summer.

He had a great knack about him. He was a handsome kid, and he had a good gab and a good line of talk.

In the First World War he became an aviator. And after the war he had this small plane, and he decided that instead of booking games by mail, he'd go out and fly to the different towns and promote the games. And he was killed in a plane accident in Oklahoma in May of 1919. It was a sad thing. Because there's no doubt in my mind that Ira Bidwell would have gone on to own a big-league ball club and been a tremendous man as far as sports were concerned.

At Central High I played just about every sport they had except track, which I didn't have time for, except maybe in an interclass meet. I was on the baseball team three years and on the basketball team three years. I was not too good as a goal shooter in basketball, but I was a pretty good guard. George Goldman was our best player.

That basketball was a terrific thing in Kansas City. Every high school in town would try to have a great team. We had some outstanding men as referees at the games. There was Ernie Quigley, who became a National League umpire, and Phog Allen, the great basketball coach at Kansas University, who retired just a few years ago.

I was also on the Central High football team in 1908, the only year they had football. I played fullback and got elected captain, but then they threw the sport out for fifteen or twenty years. One reason was that one of the young men got kicked in the head, and for a while they thought he was going to die. So they said football was too dangerous.

We played then without headgear. And we had to make five yards in three downs, and in those three downs you were supposed to put your head down and butt that line. They didn't allow you to have any forward passes. So football then was a little too rough without the head-gear. If you stumbled or slipped and kicked a man who was down, he couldn't move his head out of the way, as the play was so close in the line.

In 1909 we won the city championship in basketball and the state championship in baseball. That turned out to be the last year for baseball at Central, too—they found they couldn't make the sport pay. Anyhow, I pitched the final championship game against Joplin and won it in fifteen innings. In later years I always thought I'd pitched a shutout in that game, but I looked it up the other day and found the score was 7-6.

But the important thing was that it was for the state championship and I went fifteen innings. I think this was what got the Kansas City Blues of the American Association interested in me. They signed me to start in professional ball in 1910.

I dropped out of high school that spring. So I didn't graduate, but I did have enough credits by then to go to dental school.

Kid Nichols, an old-time pitcher who's in the Hall of Fame now, lived across the street from me then in Kansas City. He came over and gave me the best advice when I signed up to be a ballplayer.

He said, "I understand you get in a lot of trouble at school and in a lot of arguments. Now when you start out in baseball, the best thing you can do is listen to your manager. And once in a while you'll have an old player teach you. Always listen to a man. Never say, 'I won't do that.' Always listen to him. If you're not going to do it, don't tell him so. Let it go in one ear, then let it roll around there for a month, and if it isn't any good, let it go out the other ear. If it is any good after a month, memorize it and keep it."

And that's what his advice was in baseball. He said, "Now be sure you do that and you'll keep out of a lot of trouble."

7

✂ I played in professional baseball for twenty years, of which thirteen were in the National League. I was fairly good at times—my lifetime batting average for my big-league career was .284. But a lot of people seem to remember some of the stunts I pulled better than they do the ball games I helped to win.

Now comedians aren't really wanted in baseball. If you're a comedian you belong on the stage. It is never funny to a baseball owner who has a five-million-dollar investment to have a man cutting up in public. And I would like to say that I never tried anything out of the way when I was actually making a play in a regular game. It was always in an exhibition game or between plays. But I probably did too much of it. Some of it, I guess, was funny.

The one that's remembered the most was the time I came back to Ebbets Field in 1918 after being traded from Brooklyn to Pittsburgh over the winter. Those Brooklyn fans were riding me. They cheered you as long as you were playing for them, but when you went away you weren't any good, see.

One of my old Brooklyn buddies, Leon Cadore, was out

in the bullpen. He was a cutup—loved to do card tricks, loved to do coin tricks. He was very agile with his hands, and he'd caught this young sparrow in the bullpen that day. Just before my first time at bat I got it from him and put it under my cap. I could feel it moving, you know, inside there on my scalp.

So I walked up to the plate swinging three bats very hard. And the crowd yells, everybody gets excited, and they're booing me to death. Then I threw the bats down and grabbed my eye as if something was in it, and said, "Time." Cy Rigler was umpiring behind the plate, and he called time. Then I turned around to face the crowd and lifted my hat off and made a big bow. And when that bird flew out, the crowd just went, "Oh-h-h-h-h-h-h-h-h."

After the game people were saying to my old Brooklyn manager, Wilbert Robinson, "There's a guy who's crazy," and "There's a guy who thinks he's funny," and so forth. And he said, "Well, there's no use getting excited about it. He has birds in his garret, that's all."

Another thing people still talk about is something that happened to Uncle Robbie himself. And I was supposed to have been responsible for it, but I wasn't. This was on the Brooklyn club in 1915. We were training in Florida at Daytona Beach, and Ruth Law, the aviatrix, was there with this airplane. It had like two sails on it, and a lot of wires, and a rod for your feet and a rod to hold onto. Mr. Johnson, of the Endicott Johnson Shoe Company in Binghamton, was staying near there, and he paid for rides in the plane for any of us that wanted to go up.

Now a while before then Gabby Street, the old catcher, had caught a baseball that was dropped off the top of the Washington Monument. So everybody wondered whether you could catch a ball out of an airplane. And we didn't know, because which of us had even seen an airplane before? Jack Coombs, the pitcher, had been to a university, and he tried to figure out the velocity of a baseball from maybe four hundred feet in the air, and what would it weigh when it hit the ground, or was there any difference in it than when you dropped a bag of feathers.

Well, we had a trainer named Kelly. Robbie had met him at the race tracks in Baltimore with John McGraw. A trainer in those days was mostly a man that gave you rubdowns, and Kelly, no doubt, had experience at rubbing horses. Anyway, Kelly was going to go up in that plane and drop a baseball over our field. He got to fly in place of one of the ballplayers, Raleigh Aitchison. Aitchison was just married and his wife wouldn't let him go up.

The night before I was dancing with Ruth Law, and she asked me who was going to fly the next day. I told her it would be Aitchison. I didn't know about the switch then, and she never did find it out. Years later, when some writer was checking on this whole story, he wrote to Ruth Law and asked her who went up in the plane with her. She told him it was Raleigh Aitchison.

But it was Kelly. Now Kelly was in such a hurry to get to where the plane was and get back to his work before Robbie missed him that he forgot to bring along a baseball. So he just grabbed a grapefruit off a tree and took that up with him instead.

Now no matter what's been said since, I didn't know he was going to take that grapefruit. And as far as aiming it at just one man from up in the air—how could you do it?

Well, we're out on the field practicing, and the plane

comes over, and here comes this grapefruit down. Everybody thought it was a baseball being dropped and started running to get under it. But the wind carried it over to where Robinson was warming up a pitcher along the sideline. And Robbie waved everybody off and said, "Look out! I got it!"

Robbie was over fifty, and he told me later that as that thing got closer he thought his eyes must be getting blurred with age, because it looked larger than a baseball. He put his glove up and it caromed off the edge of the glove and hit him right on the chest. And he spun around and then fell over, like in a Western picture where you see an Indian that's out on a hill, and they shoot him and he goes around in a circle and falls dead.

The inside of the grapefruit had come out, and parts of it were sticking on Robbie's face. We all came running up with our mouths open, but when we saw it was a grapefruit that had hit him, everybody commenced laughing. And Robbie was burned up. He soon got rid of that trainer. He said he didn't see any fun in a big simpleton going up there and throwing a grapefruit out, though to tell the truth, a baseball might have hurt him worse than the grapefruit did.

The other teams had been calling him Round Robbie, because he was so fat and all—he had to wear a stomach band. But after this happened they called him Grapefruit Robbie. He'd get out on the coaching lines, and they'd go, "Hey, Grapefruit. Oh, Grapefruit."

Sometime later, when we were all talking about London being bombed from a zeppelin during the First World War, Robbie said, "That must be awful. Why, if a man was that high up in the air in a zeppelin, he could take a sack of peanuts. He wouldn't have to have a barrel of spikes. Say he dropped a sack of peanuts on you, you'd think it was a barrel of spikes by the time it hit you." So he still had the memory of catching that grapefruit down there at Daytona, Florida.

Then there was the one that happened in my first spring training with the Brooklyn club in 1913. We were playing an exhibition game in Pensacola, Florida, and when I went to my position in the outfield I noticed a large steel manhole out there. I lifted up the cover and saw there was a hole about four feet deep with a faucet in it, which evidently was used when they watered the field.

Along about the fifth inning I lifted the cover and got down under it in the hole. Nobody on the infield or the benches or in the stands saw me do it. I stayed there with just my eyes sticking up above the top of the hole.

Then a fly ball was hit in my direction. Everybody was surprised not to see any outfielder there, but I jumped out holding the manhole cover over my head with my left hand. I wanted to bounce the ball off the manhole cover and catch it in my glove hand. But a high wind off the Gulf began blowing the ball away from me. I had to drop that cover and grab for the ball with my hand. How I shocked the public inside that ball park that day.

I had no time to be a comedian when I went to my first professional training camp with the Kansas City Blues at Excelsior Springs, Missouri, in 1910. I was too desperate trying to win a job. I was supposed to be a pitcher, and I worked very hard. I used to run and run and run to keep the weight off, as they said I was getting too large around the body.

But the first time I went out seriously and tried to pitch, I got slaughtered. And then I tried harder, and I tightened up my muscles instead of holding them more relaxed and limber, and they hit me harder and harder.

So after that I told them I was an outfielder. Actually, I hadn't played the outfield much at all. In high school before I became a pitcher I was a third baseman and then a second baseman. But I threw left-handed, and a left-hand thrower can't play those positions in professional ball. So I thought I'd try the outfield, and I was all right until I had to back up, and then I didn't have enough experience to turn around and catch fly balls over my head.

They'd say, "Why, that stiff, why don't he turn around and go and catch the baseball?" Danny Shay, the manager, told me, "Well, you're built like a horse anyway, with that big rear end of yours. No wonder you can't field." He said, "You ought to go down and become a pool player, because your head is as hard as those ivory billiard balls they use." And every mistake I made, they'd say, "Well, there's old Billiard Ball Stengel."

In baseball you used to find your first four or five years that some of the managers were very tough. In those days they were allowed to be more tough. They figured that if the club was paying you that money, they could tell you what to do.

They would advise you to take care of yourself. Very seldom would they let you drink too much, for one thing. What you wanted to drink at that time was probably beer. They'd tell you, "Don't drink too much beer, because you'll get beer legs." They had the theory that the alcohol in there will make you heavy and fat, and if you don't perspire every day while you work out, why, you'll get too heavy at an early age.

So they used to advise the young men not to be heavy

beer drinkers. As for those who tried to drink whiskey—
at that time you could get it in a saloon for fifteen cents
a slug, but when you drank too much they would put you
out of the place. They would say, "You've drunk enough
in here, you're ruining my trade. Get out and go some
place else." And you couldn't go any place else, because
they would say, "Go back where you got it."

If a man was a drinker, they always said, "He won't
last long in baseball." But very seldom did they have to
worry much about alcoholism among the young players.
Because in bars, no one was allowed in until eighteen or
twenty-one. And if you walked in and didn't look eighteen
or twenty-one, they didn't want you eating that free lunch
they generally had going to keep business good, and the
bartender would see to it that you didn't stay in his place.

But I was talking about my first training camp with the
Kansas City Blues. If you were going to play in a top
minor league like the American Association at that time,
you had to know how to execute all the plays. They didn't
have coaches to teach the rookies, and there was nothing
like the instructional school for young players we started
before spring training beginning in 1950 when I was managing the Yankees.

But there were a couple of older players sitting around
who had big-league experience. One was Spike Shannon,
an outfielder. He was an $11,000 beauty from the Giants
—that's what he'd cost them, which was big money in
the old days. The other one was Pat Flaherty. He'd been
a big-league first baseman, pitcher and outfielder—he was
an all-around man. When the Kansas City club took its
first road trip that season, they left the three of us behind,
and those two older men worked with me. Flaherty would

hit fungos and Shannon would sit on a bench or a chair in the outfield and give me instructions.

Flaherty would hit the ball over my head, and I was supposed to run back as far as I could and then see if I could get to it. I'd miss the ball sixty feet, fifty feet, forty feet—right or left, forward or backward. But after about ten days I was getting within five or ten feet of some of them.

Flaherty could still pitch, although he couldn't pitch fast. So they put me up to the plate to hit against him. This was before there was a rule against the quick return —when a pitcher got the ball from the catcher, he could pitch it right back without any waiting if he wanted to.

So Flaherty took a big windup and pitched to me, and then when the ball came back to him he pitched it again right quick. I wasn't ready. I was looking down at the plate and getting my feet set. And he unloaded with one and hit me in the stomach and knocked me flat. And he said, "I just wanted to give you a tip. Never take your eye off the baseball."

And that's still the most important thing you could teach a ballplayer to this day. A manager that had nerve enough to do it, if he could rig up a machine that would ring a bell every time somebody wasn't watching the ball, everybody would be guilty at one time or another.

A man that I wanted to teach quick, I'd just say to him, "Watch the baseball, whether you're on the ball field or on the bench." So he watches the pitcher, watches the ball go to the plate, watches it go back. He sees all the plays at all the bases—whether the fielder tagged the man, where he threw the ball after, whether he put his foot on the bag or didn't put his foot on the bag. So therefore he becomes bright. He sees how the other players hold the ball, how they make the different plays. He knows how many times they throw bad.

It's hard to make ballplayers watch the ball like that nowadays if they're on the bench. Especially if you're in the second division. You get sleepers on there. They're thinking of something else.

That first spring I stayed with the Kansas City Blues long enough to have a lot of my old friends from Central High come out to the ball park one day and give me a good riding. We were playing the Boston Red Sox in an exhibition game before the season. Smokey Joe Wood was pitching for them. He was a Kansas City boy, and he wasn't twenty-one yet, but this was his third year in the big leagues.

Not many people know this, but he started out on a Bloomer Girls' team. In those days there were two of them that toured the small towns in Missouri and Kansas and Oklahoma. They'd get young kids who didn't have to shave, and put wigs on them to make them look like girls. Smokey Joe Wood was one of them.

Anyway, he pitched for the Red Sox in this exhibition game, and was he fast! He also had a good curve ball, and he was throwing the ball past everybody. I kept thinking they might put me up to pinch hit, but they never did. Instead, the manager gave me the job of rubbing mud on the new baseballs to take the shine off. And I also had to go and get the water bucket filled, and carry it down to the bench.

Well, these fellows I'd been to school with were sitting in the stands. They looked down and saw me and said, "Look, he's a water carrier." The man that owned the club was Gus Tebeau. So these fellows would all yell together, "Tebeau's Water Carrier. Tebeau's Water Carrier. One, two, three. Tebeau's Water Carrier." And I was never so embarrassed in my life.

I didn't get to play any games for the Blues that spring. They sent me down for experience to Kankakee, Illinois, in the Northern Association. Before I left, Pat Flaherty told me to keep practicing my fielding, and he said, "I want you to go out and learn how to slide."

I said, "I won't get a chance until next year. I trained all spring as a pitcher."

He said, "You practice sliding."

So I did my best to follow his instructions when I got to Kankakee. It's hard to find a good fungo hitter if you are in a low minor league, but I went around with this pitcher named Scheetz from Nashville, and he could hit the fly balls over my head the way I wanted. I'd go after the ball, and then throw it as far in as I could with accuracy. Then a relation of Scheetz's by the name of McTigue, who later went to the Braves as a pitcher for two or three years, would go out and pick up the ball.

And while the ball was getting back to Scheetz, I'd practice my sliding. I'd put my glove down on the grass and run and slide into it on my right side. Then I would do the same on my left side, and then I would do the same thing straight in.

People used to think I was crazy putting on a performance like that. There was an insane asylum across from the baseball field, and on the bench one day a player named Gilligan said, "Stengel is one fellow who won't be here next year."

The others said, "Why? Do you mean he's going to the big leagues?"

"No," he said, shaking his head in the direction of the

insane asylum. "I mean he's going into that building over there."

But all that practice helped me. From not being a good slider, I became one of the leading base stealers in the league. I also improved in my outfield play. Along with learning to go back for fly balls, I learned to come in and make diving catches of line drives. At first I'd dive straight forward and both elbows would hit the ground, and it would knock the ball out of my glove. Then I found a way of turning my shoulders so I could dive and get my glove under the ball without having the elbows hit first and kick it out.

My salary at Kankakee was $135 a month. I tried living at the Commercial Hotel, but that was a little too stiff for me. So I moved to a rooming house where I paid around four dollars a week. And I used to get a five-dollar meal ticket for three-fifty at McBroom's Restaurant—you could go a long way on that. And sometimes I'd get invited out to somebody's house for dinner.

When the team was home we'd pick up our mail at Mr. Hickey's place. He was the treasurer of the ball club, and we could have our mail sent in care of him. He was a mortician, and a first-class one. He had five or six coffins up on display stands, so that anyone who came in there would have something to choose from.

Well, in a game one day I was running in from center field for a short fly ball, and the second baseman was running back for it. That was Gilligan—the man who made the crack about me and the insane asylum. Now one of the worst things you can do in a ball game is to stop and let a fly ball drop. So I kept on going, and so did Gilligan, and I stepped on his foot and spiked him. That kept him out of the line-up for three days, and very nearly cost him his job.

Gilligan and a friend of his—a catcher named Boyle— hung out at Mr. Hickey's place a lot. The next time I went for my mail they were there standing around, and Gilligan said, "You big smart aleck, you know you're liable to get me fired. They're trying to get another second baseman out of Chicago. Why don't you watch what you're doing and listen? I yelled for that ball all the way."

And I said, "Is that so? All right, Duck Nose, I'll listen to you."

He did have a nose that was built something like a duck, and he didn't like that remark. He took a pop at me and knocked me right into one of those coffins that were standing there open. And that pushed the coffin off the stilts it was on. After Gilligan and his friend had knocked me all over the place, Mr. Hickey blamed me for upsetting that coffin. He decided I wasn't a very desirable youth to have around the place, and he told me, "Don't you come in and get your mail here any more." So I had to write my mother and everybody not to send my letters there.

Some of the men in that Northern Association became pretty well known in baseball. Bobby Veach, who played with Ty Cobb at Detroit, was in the outfield with me at Kankakee. Pants Rowland was the manager at Jacksonville—he's had a long career as a manager and official. A couple of men that later became famous as scouts were players in the league—Ted McGrew at Decatur and Cy Slapnicka at Muscatine.

It was all great experience while it lasted. The Northern Association started the season as a Class C league with eight teams. A couple of them had financial difficulties, and on July 9, 1910, the others reorganized and started all over again as a Class D league with six teams. It didn't last. On July eighteenth the Northern Association went out of business completely.

8

In most of the record books the start of my professional baseball career is a blank. In other words, the record books show that I played at Kankakee in 1910, but they generally don't give any figures. They think that when the Northern Association broke up that July, the records were lost too.

Well, that isn't so. There's a complete set of league statistics for 1910, and I have a copy of it. It shows that I hit .251 in fifty-nine games, and tied for fifth place in stolen bases with sixteen. I also pitched in relief in one game—I didn't get either a win or a loss.

I had half a month's pay coming to me—$67.50—when the Kankakee club went out of business. I didn't get it, so I took my uniform instead. In 1956 I happened to mention this at a birthday luncheon that was given for me in Kansas City. The story got back to Kankakee, and the Kankakee Federal Savings and Loan Association presented me with a check for $483.05—the $67.50 plus interest. I turned the check over to the Kankakee Little League.

Fortunately for me, when that league folded up in July of 1910, it didn't put me out of business as a ballplayer.

I was still the property of the Kansas City Blues, and they shifted me over to Shelbyville, Kentucky, in the Blue Grass League. And the Shelbyville franchise failed too, but the team transferred right over to Maysville, Kentucky. They said in Maysville, "We'll take you." A man there that was a plumber took the club over for the rest of the year.

We were on the road in Lexington, Kentucky, when this happened. Somebody had to go back to Shelbyville and get everybody's belongings and bring them to Maysville. They picked me to do it, and you should have seen me when I got to the Shelbyville station with all those bags. It looked like I had enough to fill a freight car. But the trainmen said, "Okay, just load them on the front here next to the engine." So the bags got to Maysville with just a little soot on them.

At Maysville they were very excited about having a professional team—they'd never had one before. I remember there would be special awards and prizes for players who did outstanding things. My batting average for sixty-nine games in the Blue Grass League was only .223, but on the last day of the season I hit a home run and won a Gem razor.

The American Association season hadn't ended yet, and from Maysville I went back to the Kansas City Blues and got in four or five games—none of the record books seem to show this, either. So in my first professional season in 1910 I played in four different cities and three different leagues.

My father had told me I had to go into something else outside the baseball season, so I started to study dentistry that fall. A fellow named Billy Brammage, who I used to play semipro ball with, said he was going over to the

Western Dental College in Kansas City, and I said, "I'll go with you."

My first two years in baseball I saved enough money for dental college after the season, and then when I made the big leagues the third year I dropped out. A man by the name of Workman, who was president of the school, said I might as well stay in baseball for a while, and then I'd have enough money to open my own office with all-white equipment if I decided to go back and become a dentist.

Another suggestion they gave me was, "Why don't you become an orthodontist? Everybody will pay to have their kids' teeth fixed. They won't always pay for their own—they'll owe for dental bills. But if you become an orthodontist, which is new now, you'll get more money and get rich, because everybody will pay for his son or for his daughter."

One thing I found out in that school was that you'd better go over something three or four times before you tried to do it. They had a demonstration exhibition to see what the students knew about extracting teeth. There were some free patients for the students to practice on, and I thought I could pull this man's tooth.

Well, first of all, I was left-handed, and I tried to do it with a right-handed instrument. And I got pretty fancy —I held it the way you'd hold your fork the first time you went into a high-class restaurant with people watching you. And then I made the mistake of not putting the chair low enough.

They'd told us, "Just twist your wrist and take the tooth out like a cork. Don't pull it, or you'll break the jaw or crack the tooth off." So I'm giving it that twist, but with the chair too high, when I got to pull up, the patient starts raising up too. And I was worried, because that boy had tears coming out of his eyes.

Finally the instructor said, "Would it do you some good to lower the chair?" So I lowered that chair down, with the whole class kind of snickering and laughing—those that knew what I'd been doing wrong and those that didn't. When I got the man down and took a hold and did that twist again, out came that tooth, and boy, I was a happy man. I guess he was too. After that the only people that would take a chance with me practicing dentistry were my parents.

I remember in the dissecting class at dental school they would have the bodies of convicts who had died at the penitentiary, and they would have you examine the mouth and the jaw, and so forth. This was a serious business, naturally. But once in a while fellows would fool around with those bodies when nobody was looking, and the first thing you knew you'd find an extra thumb in your pocket.

Once I went from the school to see my friend Harold Lederman at his father's cigar store at 1111 Grand. I shook hands with him and left an extra finger in his hand, and it almost scared him to death.

Harold is a little guy who used to live a couple of doors away from me on Park Street when I was going to the Garfield ward school, and he's still one of my best friends. He's very good company, and all his life he's been doing favors for people. Any time a kid got in trouble he would be trying to help him. He'd call up the parents, although he wasn't much more than a kid himself, and tell them what had happened. And he'd say, "Now you know he's not really a bad boy," and so on and so forth.

Harold later went into the credit jewelry business under

George Goldman, who used to be a basketball star at Central High. But when I was starting out in baseball he ran that cigar store for his father, and I used to spend a lot of my spare time there in the off season.

Well, my first year in the big leagues I found out about some stuff called cow's itch, and I brought it back to Kansas City with me. Men would come into the cigar store and play cards in the back room. A man would leave the card game and say, "Good-bye, boys." I'd say good-bye and pat him on the back, and while I was doing it I'd rub this cow's itch on his cheek and the back of his neck. We'd watch him go down the street, and all of a sudden, after about a block and a half, we'd see him commence rubbing and scratching where I'd put the cow's itch.

There was another trick we had. In the window of the cigar store there'd be fake boxes of candy on display for advertising. The window opened on a hinge, and the hinge was in the center. We'd fill one of these candy boxes with small pieces of brick wrapped in cotton, like that trick I told you I played on my brother. We'd pull the window part way open with a rope and prop the candy box up on top of the window. Then when somebody stopped to look at the candy display, we'd let go of the rope. The window would close and the candy box would drop down, sometimes right on top of the man's head.

We'd be sitting inside the store very innocent like. We'd never let on that we were watching. The man would look to see what had hit him. Sometimes he'd pick up the box and open it and see there was just broken brick in it. But half of them would sneak away with it like they were stealing something.

My second year in baseball, which was 1911, the Kansas

City Blues sent me to Aurora, Illinois, in the Wisconsin-Illinois League. The man that ran the Aurora team was Al Tebeau, a nephew of Pat Tebeau, who owned the Blues. Al Tebeau also had a gambling establishment in Aurora where you could play cards, and he had a saloon, and so forth.

So on our train trips he watched us play cards, and after he saw me playing poker he called to me the next day on the bench. He said, "You know, you look to me like you can go to the big leagues. You've got the ability to do it. But if you want to be a big leaguer, you'd better quit playing cards. Because if you don't you're going to be broke every payday. I really know. That's my bread and butter, this gambling business. And you sure can't play cards." And he cured me of poker right there.

On our road trips we'd get on the Royal Elgin train—the Blue Streak electric line. You'd go on the electric lines if you could, to Elgin and Aurora. Or you'd go to Chicago, and then you had to get off and go to another station—whichever railroad it was that went to the town where you were going.

The hotels in that league were all alike. The sheriff or the night detective would be in the lobby, and there generally would be big chairs in there where all the traveling salesmen would sit. If it was a cold spring they would all sit around the fireplace where they burned coal or wood.

The rooms were something. We always wanted a washbowl if we could get it. The first thing you'd wash was your face. Then you'd wash your ears, then you'd wash your arms. You'd go down, and then you'd put your legs in, one at a time, and wash them. There'd be more dirt on your legs after a game than anywhere else—cakes of dirt.

Some of the fellows used to wear white understockings

at the time. You'd wash them out at the ball park, if there was a hydrant there or anything, and if there wasn't you'd wash them in your room. Some guys would throw them out when they got holes in, but others would take and sew them up. They'd say, "I ain't gonna waste no ten or fifteen cents for these stockings."

At home they'd try to help you out by arranging for you to eat in a boarding house. They'd tell you, "This lady doesn't have any more rooms, but ask her if you could eat there. The meals are great." And some places the meals were terrific. How they'd feed us!

My first year in the minors I hadn't hit too much, but at Aurora in 1911 I led the league with .352, and I led it in stolen bases with fifty. Larry Sutton, a scout for the Brooklyn Dodgers, came over from Chicago to watch the Aurora club. I was going pretty well at the time, but he was partial to me because he had a superstition. He liked light-haired ballplayers. Anyway, he got the Brooklyn club to draft me from Aurora after that 1911 season.

Brooklyn started me out with Montgomery, Alabama, in the Southern Association in 1912. That was a Class A team, but they would pay me only $150 a month, where I'd been making $175 in Class D at Aurora. I was so mad I was going to quit baseball and go into dentistry or something else.

Larry Sutton talked to me. He said, "Now look. Count up the twenty-five dollars a month they've cut you. In a five-month season, you're out a hundred and twenty-five dollars. Now don't you know that a hundred and twenty-five dollars will never keep you alive? You'd be foolish to give up baseball for a hundred and twenty-five dollars. Why don't you suffer that cut and work hard down here at Montgomery, so you can move up to the big leagues and get a larger salary?" And I saw he was right, because I knew I couldn't get a job in Kansas City at that time for $125 a year, let alone $125 a month.

The manager of the Montgomery team, Johnny Dobbs, had a bird dog that he took everywhere, even on road trips. The other teams would say, "He's in love with that bird dog." And every time he went out on the coaching lines they would whistle like you do to call a dog.

There was considerable rivalry between Montgomery and the Atlanta team, which was managed by Humpty McDolan. They used to call it the McDolan Clan against the Dobbs Clan. We'd go out to the ball park in Atlanta in this little horse-drawn bus. Kid Elberfeld, a real tough old-timer who had just come down after fourteen years in the big leagues, would take this big black bat and sit out on the step. And if people ran up to the bus while we were riding out, he'd swipe at them with that bat.

Kid Elberfeld played shortstop. He said to me, "You want to get to the big leagues, watch me." And I want to tell you, he'd get you there or get you in jail. Or get you out of jail. He'd stand up at the plate and get in the way of the ball so he could take his base, and then to make it look good he'd run out and throw his bat at the pitcher. He'd say, "You threw at me on purpose!"

He tried to teach me how to execute the different plays when I was on the bases—the hit and run, and so forth. He could really hit and run with you from second base. He'd make me take a big lead off second, so the shortstop would have to run over to hold me on, then I'd go to steal third, so the third baseman would have to cover his base. Then Elberfeld would stroke the ball through that big hole with his short bottle bat.

In one holiday doubleheader I had a red-hot day. I got

something like six hits in eight times at bat. But every time I got on I thought I could steal, and I must have thought that to steal a base I had to look at it, because I kept looking at the next base instead of at Kid Elberfeld, who was hitting behind me. At least three times he hit line drives that were caught on the fly, and I'd be running with my eyes on that next base. I'd make beautiful runs and beautiful slides, but in the meantime they'd be doubling me off the base I'd just left.

The last time it happened I started from second base, and as I rounded third, who should I see coming down the line toward me but Elberfeld. Instead of running to first base he'd started after me, waving his bat over his head and yelling. He chased me all the way back around those bases.

A scout from the Washington ball club named Mike Kayhoe was watching that doubleheader. Some people asked him afterward what he thought of me.

He said, "Gee, Stengel handles that bat well. And I'll tell you another thing, he can run and field, and he can throw. He's just what anybody needs on a ball club, except for one thing."

And they said, "What's that?"

He said, "He is a dandy ballplayer, but it's from his shoulders down."

In other words, I was what they used to call a "billiard head." Or they'd say, "That boy is concrete." And they had names like "rock." If you made a stupid play out on the field, they'd ask, "Say, were you born in Rock Island?"

Even so, I had a pretty good year at Montgomery. I hit .290 and stole a lot of bases. Brooklyn called me up to play the last part of the 1912 season with them.

Kid Elberfeld thought that was great, and he insisted that I go up to Brooklyn in big-league style. He said, "You can't go up there with that bag you're carrying." We used to have thick cardboard suitcases, and if you got caught out with one in a hard rain, all you had left was a handle. I thought my old suitcase would do for the two or three weeks that were left, but Elberfeld made me buy myself a new leather bag for $17.50. And he said I also had to get a new suit, and buy wine for the fellows who saw me off.

I hated to put out all that money, as I wasn't making a very big salary, but I really didn't care too much. The big leagues were what I'd been aiming at from the time I signed into professional ball, and now, less than three years after I started, I was getting my chance.

✄ When I went up to New York City to
join the Brooklyn Dodgers in September of 1912, the first
place I hit was a hotel at 47th and Broadway, where
my Uncle Charlie Jordan from Davenport, Iowa, was
staying. He introduced me at the desk, and I checked in.
The next morning I set out to find the Brooklyn ball park.
They were playing in Washington Park then; Ebbets Field
didn't open until the next year.

I left at eight o'clock in the morning and it took me
about four hours to get there. I had to ride more ele-
vateds and trolley cars. I walked into the office and told
them who I was, and the man said, "What are you doing
here?" He didn't know I'd been told maybe a month before to report to Brooklyn at the end of the Southern Association season. So I explained that, and he said, "Well,
go down to the clubhouse."

It was a very dilapidated clubhouse, with just a
wooden floor. They had let it run down because they
were building a new ball park. When I got in there I
didn't know who to talk to but Zach Wheat, an outfielder who had lived in Kansas City, Kansas. When I
told him I was from Kansas City, Missouri, and so on and

so forth, he took charge of me and put me in the locker next to him.

The game wasn't going to start for another couple of hours, and the Brooklyn manager, Bad Bill Dahlen, hadn't come out yet. So one or two of the players said, "Let's start a crap game." I stood around and watched them, and finally I got into it, despite what Al Tebeau had advised me in Aurora—that I had no ability as a gambler and should stay away from it.

I had only about forty or fifty dollars to my name, after buying that suitcase and the wine and everything when I left Montgomery. I lost some, then began to get it back when my turn came to shoot the dice.

And then in came the manager. He saw all of us down there on the floor, heads in a circle, and he said, "What do you men think you're doing? Don't you know there's a ball game on in this town?" And he looked at me and he said, "Throw those dice down. What did you come up here to do?"

I said, "To play ball."

He said, "Well, if you're gonna play ball, you get out on that field. We didn't bring you up here for a crap-shooter."

And I said, "No, I don't think you did."

Then he gave me the information that I was going to start in center field that afternoon. This was September 17, 1912. I'll never forget that game. We were playing Pittsburgh. Claude Hendrix, who used to play with me on that traveling semipro team, the Kansas City Red Sox, was their starting pitcher.

The first time up I hit a single. The second time my manager gave me the bunt sign and I fouled the ball off. I saw that the third baseman was running in on me, and also the first baseman and the pitcher, so on the second pitch I swung away instead of bunting. But I'd forgotten to look at my manager. He hadn't taken the bunt sign off. But he didn't say too much to me about hitting away when I was supposed to bunt, because I was new and also because I got another base hit.

Well, I got hits the third and fourth times too. When I came up for my fifth turn they had a left-handed pitcher in there, which can be tough on a left-handed hitter like myself. Fred Clarke, the Pittsburgh manager, yelled, "All right, you big busher, now let's see what you can do."

So I went up there and stood at the plate right-handed, which I very seldom did, because I was never adept at hitting from that side. If the pitcher, Sherry Smith, had gotten two strikes on me, I'd have had to switch back. But he walked me. So that gave me a perfect day at bat in my first game in the big leagues.

In the outfield Zach Wheat was supposed to look after me, and when Hans Wagner came up to bat for Pittsburgh, Wheat said, "Play back." I said, "Well, I'm back pretty far now." He said, "Better play back deeper." I went back another five feet, and he still hit the ball over my head in center field. So I found out in a hurry who Hans Wagner was.

Two days later I was playing against the Chicago Cubs, with Tinker to Evers to Chance—that famous double-play combination. I went down and slid into second base, and Evers took and threw that ball and hit me with it.

I looked up at him, and he made out like I'd been going to cut him. He said, "Why, you big busher, you. I'd like to see you come down here and start anything. If you ever cut me, you'll never play another game in the big leagues." And for a while there I didn't get along very good with Johnny Evers.

Anyhow, I got off to a pretty good start there at the end of the 1912 season. I got all those hits in my first game. Then I made two good catches. Then I stole a couple of bases. My batting average for seventeen games was .316.

So everybody said, "Here's the new phenom in baseball." They thought I was better than Zach Wheat, a great left-handed hitter. They thought I was better than Jake Daubert, the great Brooklyn first baseman.

But by the next year the other clubs knew my batting weaknesses, and I didn't do as well—.272 in 124 games. I swung too hard at a ball, and I had too long a stride. A change-up used to get me, and I was weak on a ball that was high inside. I'd get hit on the fist with it more than I got hit on the good part of the bat. And I was weak against certain great left-handers, like Jim Vaughn of the Cubs and Eppa Rixey of Philadelphia. They threw me a lot of curves, and then I'd start looking for the curve and the fast ball would go by me.

We also had a great left-handed pitcher on our own club, Nap Rucker. He was very graceful—everything he did was in rhythm. He had a beautiful-looking curve, and he also had a beautiful fast ball. In batting practice he'd say, "See if you can get a hit off me," and I couldn't do it. But it was good practice.

He had me in a quandary when I came up to the big leagues. I'd never seen anybody that had that big a curve. You'd fall down to get away from it, and then it would break over the plate, and you'd be embarrassed. And I was very glad I didn't have to hit against Nap Rucker in regular games.

I thought I was a good slider when I broke in—I'd led minor leagues in base-stealing—but my first Brooklyn manager, Bill Dahlen, showed me how to improve. He could slide in and just tip the base and spring straight up.

He used to roll his stockings over his knees like a doughnut, so he would have sort of a ball under each knee. Then when he slid, that raised his leg off the ground, and he rarely got a strawberry, which is when you take the skin off your leg by scraping it.

In those days you used to get quite a few strawberries from sliding. Nowadays some of the ballplayers do so little sliding they go five or six years without even wearing sliding pads. But that eventually makes a man get injured. He doesn't want to slide and get a strawberry, so he comes into a base standing up, and his spikes catch in the ground. And he either sprains an ankle or breaks it.

I generally got a number of strawberries when I was playing. I know Babe Ruth used to get them almost every day. Then he'd take a strip of toilet paper and stick it on there at night, so his pajama trousers wouldn't rub against it, and when he got up in the morning a scab would have formed. That was the quickest way and the safest way we had to heal strawberries in those days, and it was Ruth's method for a number of years.

But I was talking about 1913. I think that was the year we went over to play a special exhibition game with the Newark club. One of the events before the game was, they turned a greased hog loose on the field. Whoever caught him would get a ten-dollar prize. We were being paid fifty dollars apiece to play in this game, which was a lot of money for an exhibition, but I didn't understand that. I thought it was fifty dollars to be split among the whole team.

Most of the boys said, "I ain't going to chase that greased hog," but there were about six of us that decided to try for the ten-dollar prize. So we took after that hog. He kept getting away from us—he'd go so far and then stop and turn the other way—but finally I saw my chance. I dove for him, and he forgot to skip to the right or the left, and I got a hold of his hind legs. He eventually slipped away, but I'd held him longer than anybody else, so I won the ten dollars.

Now this was mosquito season in New Jersey. And when those big mosquitoes started buzzing me, with that grease smear on my uniform, the other guys wouldn't let me sit on the bench with them.

After the game Zach Wheat got us to go over to this restaurant that all the ballplayers liked that had ever played in Newark. And the man that owned the restaurant said, "I'll tell you what I'm going to do. I'm going to give you a bottle of champagne on the house for every bottle you men buy."

I had seldom done any drinking before. Once at the end of the season at Central High some of the fellows bought a little barrel of beer—about a sixteenth of a barrel—and we went over to a fellow's house and drank it. Then there was the wine Kid Elberfeld made me buy when I left Montgomery. Now I had to pay five dollars for a bottle of Mumm's champagne, and I didn't want to get robbed, so I drank it.

It turned out to be a little too much for me, and also for a player from the South named Frank Allen. The bad part was when we went back to New York on this subway

train, the Manhattan Transfer. It was hot and stuffy
down there. I wasn't used to it and Allen wasn't used to
it.

Zach Wheat didn't want us to get sick in front of everybody, so he took us between two cars, and a big gust of
wind came up—we were two terrible-looking sights when
we got into the station. And I cut out being a drinking
man.

Near the end of that 1913 season I tore my shoulder.
It happened when I went to catch a ball and slipped, and
then tried a quick throw. Over the winter I went to a
Y.M.C.A. to work out, and I couldn't throw. I was afraid I
might not be able to play big-league ball any more, so I
took an opportunity to go down in late winter and be a
baseball coach at Mississippi University—Ole Miss. John
Driver, who had been one of my coaches at Central High,
was running the athletic teams down there.

I worked with those college boys for several weeks, and
they seemed to take a liking to me. When I wanted to talk
to them in the evenings, they'd invite me into their frater-
nity houses. In later years I was made an honorary alum-
nus of the school. I was given a little emblem of Ole Miss,
and the way they've been doing in football these last
few years I'm glad to have it.

Well, my arm came around there in 1914 and I didn't
stay through their season, but I noticed they won their
state championship. And when I went from Ole Miss to the
Brooklyn training camp at Augusta, Georgia, that spring,
I think that's when one of my nicknames started—"The
Ole Perfesser."

That year Wilbert Robinson became the Brooklyn
manager. He switched me from center field to right field.
He decided that Hi Myers, who had come up from

Newark, was fleetfooted enough to be a good center fielder, and he thought I had the arm to play right field.

I remember him telling the writers about it in the hotel at Augusta. There were three writers with us from Brooklyn papers, and two from New York papers. It was a rainy day, and Robbie had to give them some news. He was in a room with them that was generally used as a display room by traveling salesmen. The writers had their typewriters there and everything, and three of them had this corn liquor. I was rooming next door with Otto Miller, and I could hear them through the wall.

Robbie said, "I'll tell you why he is going to be a right fielder. Stengel is left-handed. Now if you're in right field and going toward the foul line, a right-hand-throwing right fielder has to make a complete turn around to throw, or else he has to reverse backwards. But a left-handed man don't have to turn. He can get the throw away quicker and more accurately."

Well, one of the writers, after he got back to his own room where his wife was asleep, he wanted to prove it to himself. He told us about this the next day. He's got a lot of this corn liquor working on him now, and he wants to know, why is a left-handed man better in right field? So he stands in front of the looking glass with a lamp burning, and he's moving his left arm and making motions like he's in right field and trying to throw out a man going from first to third. And he's throwing to second, and throwing to home.

His wife wakes up and sees him going through all these motions. She says, "So you've finally come to it. I told you you were drinking too much. I told you you'd be seeing snakes soon."

Anyhow, I became a right fielder for Robinson. Later

on, in 1917, I got thirty assists to lead the league. One reason was that I charged the ball and got rid of it quick. The second was that I used to go out like in hand-ball and practice catching balls off the concrete right-field wall at Ebbets Field. I used to take and throw balls against it and get used to the bounces.

In games Hi Myers would come over from center field and back me up at the wall. I could go and jump up like I was going to catch the ball, and if I didn't, he'd catch it off the wall. Or I would jump against the wall and then turn back and catch it. If three men were on base, we could generally jam somebody up. One of the three men would forget to run or be afraid I was going to catch it, and we would get him on the bases.

Wilbert Robinson was a lot of fun to work for. On the bench they used to have arguments about corn. The farm boys would argue about how many bushels of corn you could grow to the acre. And the boys from the corn coun-try—Illinois and Kansas and Missouri and those different states—would get on the boys from states that were poor for corn. And Uncle Robbie would be right in the argu-ment.

One day the corn argument was going, and we had a six-run lead, and then the other team started a rally and finally won the game. And Robbie decided it was be-cause the players were talking about corn instead of keeping their minds on the game. So he held a meeting in the clubhouse afterward, and he said, "From now on there will be no more corn arguments from you fellows living in these different states." But he should have said it to himself.

Each player in the old days thought his home state was the greatest for everything. And there would be arguments between Northern boys and Southern boys about the Civil War. And when they would call a Southern fellow a Confederate—watch out! He'd go right after them. Anything went then. And the Northern boy too.

I had a little trouble with a fellow at Brooklyn myself. This was a pitcher named Whitey Appleton. He was a tough guy from Texas and I was supposed to be a tough guy from Missouri. But our dispute had nothing to do with where we came from. He didn't like the way I was playing behind him in right field. I always seemed to do poorly when Appleton would pitch, although I was starring in some of the other games.

One day I made a very bad play behind him. That night I was coming back from Coney Island and just about to go into my apartment building when Appleton came along with four or five other players. Now he could be very entertaining on train trips. He would imitate animals, and drive those porters half crazy looking for a dog or a cat in a berth. He was what we called a "fun box" most of the time. But this night he was mad. And he took a crack at me and knocked me into a window.

A Salvation Army band was coming down the street, so we went upstairs in the building and had it out. It ended up with us tumbling down the stairs together. We were all banged up. The same doctor sewed us both up. The next day I couldn't get my straw hat on, and he also had to wear a cap.

Out at the ball park we told them that a gang of Giant rooters had jumped us in a subway station—the Giants and Brooklyn were tremendous rivals, naturally. But the true story eventually got out, and then the owner, Mr. Ebbets, came in the clubhouse and made a speech about how bad it was to have friction between ballplayers on the team.

In later years as a manager I always tried to keep those fights from happening, because when you're in a pennant race you don't want players to cripple each other. If two players don't get along they should stay away from each other off the field. They don't even have to speak to each other, as long as they speak during the ball game.

It was that way at Brooklyn for a time with Jeff Pfeffer and me. He was another pitcher I didn't play as well for as I should. He was a right-hander who threw the cross fire overhanded, and he had wonderful control. He was always fooling Cravath and the good hitters.

He was a big, sarcastic fellow. He told me, "You're making too many mistakes." One time with Pfeffer pitching I went to catch a ball in right field with men on third and second. I knew the man on third was so fast I couldn't throw him out at home. So I let him go, which merely tied the score, and threw the ball to third to get the other man. But the third baseman stumbled when he was backing up to catch the ball, and it went on through. There was nobody behind him to cut it off, as Pfeffer was backing up home plate. So the runner from second went all the way around and scored too, which cost us the game.

Pfeffer didn't think that was a very good play, and nobody else thought it was a very good play, and it wasn't a very good one. For two or three years he and I didn't talk to each other. But later on we became immense and amazing friends. And I got so I could play better for him.

Well, the Brooklyn club under Wilbert Robinson improved. In 1915 we finished third, and in 1916 we were fighting for the pennant against Philadelphia, which had won the year before, and also against Boston, which had won in 1914.

The Philadelphia club had great pitchers like Alexander and Rixey. They had Cravath in the outfield—they had sluggers who could really hit that ball. They had a good infield, in which Dave Bancroft was on short and Luderus was on first base. And they had Killefer catching.

On our club Jake Daubert was possibly the best first baseman in either league. He could hit a ball, and he could bunt. He could bunt it down the third-base line and it would reverse just like a cue ball on a billiard table—he could slice at it with his bat and get that reverse twist on it. At second base George Cutshaw was a very good man. At shortstop we had Ivy Olson and Ollie O'Mara.

On our pitching staff we had Jeff Pfeffer and Rube Marquard and Sherry Smith and Jack Coombs; Nap Rucker was getting near the end of his time. Chief Meyers and Otto Miller were the catchers.

In the outfield our best man was Zach Wheat. He was a terrific line-drive hitter. He often hit in bad luck, because with the dead ball, the outfielders could play short and catch a lot of those line drives that were hit over the infield.

Near the end of the season it got down to where we had a half-game lead over Philadelphia, and we were playing them a big morning-afternoon doubleheader in Brooklyn on September thirtieth. They won the morning game to move ahead of us, and for the afternoon game they had Grover Alexander, one of the greatest pitchers in the world—he won thirty-three games and pitched sixteen shutouts that year.

10

When I first came into the National League I ruined a no-hit game for Grover Alexander with a single in the eighth inning. And he never did get a no-hitter in all the years he pitched. But as time went on I found I couldn't hit him at all. Just on rare occasions would I get a base hit off Alexander.

Well, when he pitched against us at the end of 1916 with first place at stake, and they scored a run in the first inning, I said, "I'll step in at that plate if it kills me." And I got a lucky hit off the handle of the bat in our half of the first and eventually scored the tying run.

In the fifth inning the score was still 1-1, and it looked like a tremendous storm was coming up. Here came the wind, here came the cold, and everybody in the park commenced putting their collars up. I stepped in at the plate and he hit me on the handle of the bat again, and I hit a long, high fly. The wind got a hold of this baseball and there it soared, and it dropped just outside the right-field fence on Bedford Avenue.

I was so tickled that I stopped down at first base and chuckled and yelled and looked over that fence. Then I stopped at second base and brushed it off with my cap. I brushed off third base with my cap. And some of the players on that Philadelphia team were calling me every name you ever heard of.

Later on I got another hit and scored another run off a relief pitcher. We won the game 6-1, and went on from there to take the pennant. Then we went into the 1916 World Series against the Boston Red Sox.

To get more money out of the Series, we played in the new National League park in Boston, which seated over 40,000 people, instead of in the smaller park of the Red Sox. And they raised the prices. Ebbets Field only seated about 22,000—they raised the prices there too.

Ernie Shore pitched the opening game in Boston. Ty Cobb, the big American League star, was up there to see the Series, and I asked him, "How would you hit this man, Ty?"

He said, "If I was you, I'd get in front of home plate, because he keeps the ball low. And if you get in front of home plate you'll hit it higher, and that'll make it skip through the infield. You'll want the ball skipping like a rock on water. So you try to lift the ball."

I did what he said and I got two hits off Shore, but we lost the game, 6-5. I did the same thing in the third game and got a hit off Carl Mays, who pitched straight underhand—he'd give you a bowling throw. We won that time, 4-3.

That was the only game we did win. In the second game Babe Ruth, who was a pitcher then, beat us 2-1 in fourteen innings. I didn't play—Robbie knew I couldn't hit a left-hander like Ruth.

The Red Sox had a number of great players. Tris Speaker was injured and couldn't be in the Series, but they still had Harry Hooper in the outfield, and he made some amazing plays. And Duffy Lewis—he certainly did agitate us up at the plate. He'd raise his front leg up high, like he was going to swing hard, and then he'd bunt and cross us up.

After we took the third game, they won the next two. So we lost the World Series, four games to one. We thought we should have done better. I remember all winter in Kansas City I would tell people, "They were lucky. We can beat that club."

Well, we played them a number of exhibition games the next spring, and they kept on beating us. They had the same great players, and they had the same methods of pitching and the same methods of blocking you off at the plate. And they put on the same kind of hit-and-run plays. And that was a good lesson for me, because it showed me how good they really were.

From winning the pennant in 1916 the Brooklyn club dropped to seventh place in 1917. I think one reason was that the owner, Mr. Ebbets, cut some salaries, and there were three or four men that held out and didn't get to train properly. It was like what the Yankee owners did a couple of years ago. After we won the world championship in 1958 they did some salary-cutting, and then we had our bad year in 1959.

Back there in 1917 Mr. Ebbets said, "I owe for Ebbets Field." But he also owed the men that did well on the field and won a pennant for him, and he didn't show them much partiality.

Take myself, as one example. In 1915 Mr. Ebbets had raised me to about $5300 to keep me from going over to the Federal League, which started up that year in competition with the American and National Leagues. The Federal League folded up after 1916, and for 1917 he sent me a contract calling for a $1300 cut. And this was after I'd starred in the World Series, with a .364 batting average in my four games.

I wrote back like a big smart aleck, "Dear Charlie. Received the contract but knew it wasn't mine when I saw the figures. You must have sent me Red Monahan's contract by mistake."

Red Monahan was the bat boy. I know it was a mistake for me to get that smart. Mr. Ebbets got mad and sent me another contract with a $1700 cut. I finally ended up taking the $1300 cut.

As I told you before, I didn't do so well in 1917. I hit .257, and Brooklyn traded George Cutshaw and myself to Pittsburgh the next year for Burleigh Grimes, Al Mamaux and Chuck Ward. Pittsburgh gave me the same salary Mr. Ebbets had cut me to. I started pretty well in 1918 and went to see the owner, Barney Dreyfuss, about a raise. Hugo Bezdek, the manager, suggested it.

I said, "Mr. Dreyfuss, do you realize that this is my sixth big-league year but I'm playing for my third-year salary in the big leagues—the salary I got back in 1914? And yet I was traded here as a star. For heaven's sake, I want more money. That was my trouble with the last club."

He said, "More money? How do I know you're that good?"

I said, "I must have been, or you wouldn't have traded for me."

And he said, "You didn't do it for me. Show me you're that good this year."

He always had an answer for everything. If you weren't hitting .300 but doing a lot of other things to help the club, he'd say, "Wait till you hit .300." But if you hit over

.300 he'd say, "Your fielding's bad," or, "You're throwing bad." Or he'd say, "Why don't you do some base-running? Let's do something else. You're just up there hitting for yourself, and you're just up there selfish. Let's get some more of these men around and drive in some more runs."

That time I asked him for a raise, we had gotten beaten the day before, 1-0. He said, "You want more money? You know what I want? I want more runs."

Now we'd lost that 1-0 game on a handle hit that went right through the infield where nobody could touch it. And I said, "Look, you can't kick on a thing like that. Don't you know that man won that game against us on a handle hit?"

And he said, "Well, if it was a handle hit, then give me some of them handle hits. That's what I want, hits that score runs."

Another time we lost a 1-0 game to the Giants in the Polo Grounds. Wilbur Cooper pitched for us. He very seldom walked a man. This day he walked only one, but then came an error and a base hit and they scored their run.

I was standing with Cooper on the platform at the elevated station afterward, and he was still sick at losing a game like that. We were waiting for another player to finish dressing and join us. Then along came Dreyfuss. He stepped on a train, and just before they shut the doors he called to Cooper, "You and your old base on balls!"

Cooper was so mad he ran over to argue with him, but the doors closed and the train took off before he could get in a word.

Dreyfuss was a very bright man. He kept the park clean, kept it green, kept it like the lawns around Pitts-

burgh. He wouldn't allow an advertising sign in the place
—he wanted everything beautiful and picturesque. He
would have made a great commissioner of baseball.

I played only the first part of the 1918 season with
Pittsburgh. After thirty-nine games I went into the Navy.
The First World War was on, and I expected to be
drafted anyway, but I speeded it up.

It came about like this. We had a young umpire in the
National League at that time named Harris. He was
bothering me, and to tell the truth I was bothering him. It
started when a dispute came up in Pittsburgh and I got
into it, and he said, "You can't kick here. You're not the
captain."

I said, "I'm half-captain on this team." Of course, there
wasn't any such thing—Zeb Terry was the captain—but
Harris had to go and ask the other umpire to be sure.

The next day I started in from right field on an argument and he kept trying to wave me off, but he couldn't,
because I backed all the way in with my face to the
bleachers. I backed right in to home plate and started
talking before he could put me out.

Then came a game in New York. I was on first base with
one out and Cutshaw hit a double-play ball. I was an easy
out at second, but the play at first was close, and Cutshaw
was arguing with Harris about it. I started trotting over
to my position in right field. Harris thought I was coming to join in the argument at first base, and he ordered
me out of the game.

So I had to go to the clubhouse, which was out in
center field in the Polo Grounds. As I walked out there
I took my shirt off and carried it over my shoulder. I had
a woolen undershirt on—I was more dressed than those
chorus girls in the shows—but the next day I got a tele-

gram from the league president notifying me that I was being fined fifty dollars for my shocking conduct in disrobing on the ball field.

Well, I pinned that telegram around my sleeve like a mourning band and went up to the plate with it. That caused more disturbance. I figured that this time I'd draw something like a two-hundred-dollar fine and ten days' suspension, so I said to myself that night, "Why don't I go enlist?" And I enlisted in the Navy in Brooklyn.

My brother and everybody said later that showed how smart I was, because to keep from paying a two-hundred-dollar fine I gave up a salary of about four thousand a year for Navy pay of fifteen dollars a month.

They kept me right at the Brooklyn Navy Yard and gave me the job of managing their ball team. One day we were playing a game at Prospect Park and I asked a boy to hold my money for me. I had about thirty dollars with me, and there was no place to lock it up, and I didn't want to leave it in the dressing room.

Well, I got a hit and got to second base and looked around, and you know where that boy was that was holding my money? He was way at the other end of Prospect Park, wheeling off on a bicycle. So I lost another thirty dollars right there.

I had Jimmy Hickman with me on that Navy team—he'd played with me at Brooklyn—and we were very successful. I was a schedule picker. We played teams off the ships that came in there. I wouldn't play the battleship *Pennsylvania* because they had Rabbit Maranville. I'd play those shipwreck clubs—any ship that came in there from six months at sea, I'd play them within two or three days before they got over being seasick.

I was called in by Captain Stone, the man that controlled that Naval District, and he said to me, "You're doing a great job with this team." Then he said, "I'll give you a chance to advance in the Navy." And he started me on advancement to be an officer. As far as I worked up to was commissary steward. Then the armistice came and I was able to get out of the Navy.

I went back, naturally, with the Pittsburgh club in 1919. I still wasn't satisfied with my salary. So we were playing the Giants one day—everybody always wanted to beat the Giants, and I was crazy to beat them myself. I was playing right field, and a ball was hit out there on a line. I charged in and reached down for it, and the ball hit me on the right leg between the knee and the ankle.

I never saw which way it bounced. I thought it went to the right and began chasing over in that direction, but actually it had caromed off the other way toward the foul line. So I was running away from the ball, and two men were on base, and everybody scored. That lost us the ball game.

Some of the fans thought I deliberately ran the opposite way on the ball, and I was a loafer and a cheat. The workers in the steel mills were making good money in Pittsburgh then, and they'd be out in the bleachers and give you the best going-over you ever heard in your life. There was only one man out there that was my friend. He'd always cheer for me, and every day he'd bring me out a stick of candy or something before the ball game.

Anyhow, when I went out to right field the next day the fans started booing me terrifically. I went over to the bleachers—these were very small bleachers they had, before the park was rebuilt. I turned around to them and said, "Please don't yell at me that loud. I am not strong any more. I don't get much money and I don't get enough to eat."

And that burned them up. They didn't see any humor in it. As I told you, they didn't want you to be a comedian in those days. If you had a bad day, you were wasting your time with comedy, because your manager and your players and the public didn't like it.

I played with Pittsburgh until August of 1919 and was hitting .293 when they traded me over to Philadelphia for George Whitted. I wired the Philadelphia club, "There's not enough money here. Will need more to go over there." The Philadelphia owner, William Baker, wired back, "There's not much money here." So I wired him, "If there isn't enough money in Philadelphia I will be in Kansas City, Missouri."

And I went back home and stayed out the rest of the season. That was one of the times I thought about quitting baseball and going back to dentistry. In the meantime I organized a barnstorming team and took it out through Kansas and the Oklahoma oil fields and on to the West Coast.

The tour was arranged by a man that had a Bloomer Girls' team. As I remember, his name was Logan Galbreath. He booked the games for us and he took seventy-five per cent of the receipts, but out of that he had to pay our traveling expenses, plus a guarantee of something like five hundred dollars a game. So when we played in a little town, he sometimes wouldn't even break even.

We kept on going after the regular baseball season ended, and I added some big-league players to the team. I had Irish Meusel, who was with the Phillies then, and his brother Bob Meusel, who was headed for the Yankees.

One of the things I remember is going to an Army

base in Douglas, New Mexico, and playing their team two games. This team had mostly come from service in the Philippines, and they had some great colored players. They had a pitcher named Grogan—next to Satchel Paige, he was the best colored pitcher I ever saw—and a shortstop named Moore. They were as good as any major-leaguers, but colored players couldn't be in the big leagues then. Grogan ended his career in the Negro leagues with the Kansas City Monarchs.

Now when I broke into baseball years and years ago we used to have Irish and German and Polish players. And then the greatest players came from the South. Then they came from Texas, and then they came from Chicago.

Today it's the colored player. He's a good runner, and he's very quick with his wrists. He's the best hitter. The Italians are the second best hitters. The Polish player is sometimes slow and sluggish swinging the bat. The Germans are passing out, the race has gotten mixed up so much, and it's the same with the Irish. They don't talk and act like the ones did that had just come from Ireland.

Anyhow, we managed to beat this Army team with the good colored players in Douglas, New Mexico, in 1919. In one game we did it with a pitcher by the name of Gaynor from the Pacific Coast League. He threw the shine ball, but I advertised it as his mystery ball. They were familiar down there with the Mexican drink called tequila, which is made from the juice of the cactus plant, and I said, "He uses the juice of the cactus plant, and the ball does a mysterious twitch."

Actually, what Gaynor had was a small piece of emery paper stitched into his glove, and some paraffin on his pants leg. He'd rough up one side of the ball with the emery paper, and then he'd rub the ball on his pants and slick up the other side with the paraffin. That was how you threw the shine ball. You could get a terrific break on it—it would jump to the right or jump to the left. This Army team had never seen the shine ball before, and they couldn't do anything with it.

Well, I did a lot of that barnstorming while I was in baseball. But except for this one time in 1919 it was always after the season. We had a fairly successful tour that year, but I had to admit it wasn't like playing in the big leagues. And in 1920 I went back to the National League in Philadelphia.

11

✂ With the Philadelphia club in 1920 there was another time I learned I'd better not get too smart on the ball field. On our way North from spring training I made several poor plays in one of the exhibition games. Gavvy Cravath was the manager. He had a bad cold, and I didn't think he'd come out the next day to a game we had in Birmingham. So when we got out to the ball park, I put my pants on backwards for a joke and wore them that way during practice.

And Cravath did come out. He wasn't in uniform, but he'd decided to watch from the grandstand. And when he saw me, he said, "Well, I'm not surprised that you would dress backwards. You've been doing everything else backwards down here."

I ended up having a fair season in 1920—I hit .292. The next year the manager was Wild Bill Donovan. He'd been a pitcher, and he wanted his catchers to be good at handling pitchers. We had this catcher by the name of Frank Bruggy, who was a sheriff from somewhere in New Jersey, and he looked like an old-time bartender, with his big stomach and his red face. And Donovan worked him very hard. Bruggy had a Stutz car, and he used to hate to give Donovan a ride in it after a ball game, because Donovan would spend the whole time telling him what he'd done wrong.

Right before the season we had to play a city series game with Connie Mack's team, the Philadelphia Athletics, and Donovan was very anxious to make a good showing. Well, our first pitcher went out there, and bing, bing, bing—Donovan had to take him out. With the next pitcher it was the same way. It wasn't all the pitchers' fault. It was one of those days when we couldn't seem to get to any of the balls in the outfield, and the infielders were having trouble too.

Bruggy was catching, and Donovan kept yelling to him from the bench, "Mix 'em up! Mix 'em up!" So Bruggy called for every different pitch he could think of, and still the Athletics kept hitting them safe. And Donovan kept yelling, "Mix 'em up!"

Finally Bruggy called time. He turned so Donovan could hear him, and he yelled to the pitcher, "If you have anything else in your repertoire, please deliver it!" And that was pretty fancy language for Bruggy to use.

On the Philadelphia club at that time we had Lee Meadows, a very good pitcher who wore glasses. He was our Saturday pitcher—with no Sunday baseball in Pennsylvania then, that was when they drew the biggest crowds.

One day with Meadows pitching we were playing St. Louis. Branch Rickey was their manager. They had men on second and third with two out in the ninth and Rogers Hornsby, the greatest right-hand hitter in the National League, at bat. Our manager ordered Meadows to give

Hornsby an intentional walk—he put up four fingers so that everybody could see. I was out in right field, and I was hoping Meadows would walk Hornsby, because that was what I thought the situation called for.

But Meadows reared back and threw the first pitch over for a strike. So Hornsby leveled off for the next pitch, and Meadows threw a fast ball behind his head. That was one and one. Then Meadows broke a curve ball over the plate for strike two.

After that he threw ball two behind Hornsby's head, and ball three behind his head. Now Meadows thought he could get Hornsby on a curve ball for the third strike, but Hornsby stepped into it and hit the darnedest line drive I ever saw. It went out there just about three feet off the ground, but it carried all the way to the left fielder, and he caught it to end the game.

As Meadows went into the clubhouse he had to pass by Branch Rickey, and Rickey said, "Young man, you'll pay for that some day."

Anyhow, that was the roughest I ever saw a man pitched to in the major leagues. But the biggest thing was what Hornsby did, after having all those fast balls thrown behind his head. Instead of falling away from the plate on that last curve ball, he stepped in and hit a tremendous line drive.

I hit close to .300 during my time in Philadelphia, but it was a tail-end club under Cravath in 1920 and a tail-end club under Donovan in 1921. Then in July of 1921 I got a break. They made a deal to send me and Johnny Rawlings to the New York Giants.

I'd hurt my back a week before, but when they told me about the trade in the dressing room I must have jumped about six feet high. They said, "We thought you had a bad back," and I said, "I don't have a bad back now," and I jumped clean over the rubbing table.

I went right up to join the Giants in Boston that night. I didn't even wait for Rawlings to finish packing. The Giants were a club fighting for the pennant, and I wasn't going to give John McGraw a chance to change his mind about the deal.

I didn't get to play many games for the Giants the rest of that season, because to tell the truth, in spite of the way I jumped over that rubbing table, I did have a bad back. The Giants won the pennant and beat the Yankees in the 1921 World Series, and I didn't get in the Series at all.

So I made it a point that I was going to be in great shape when I went to spring training at San Antonio in 1922, and I was in great shape. McGraw worked us hard. He'd sit on a chair in front of the boxes behind home plate and watch the whole workout. He wouldn't allow us to stand around the cage between turns at batting practice, the way I'd done on some clubs. You were supposed to bunt the last ball, then run and circle the bases, then go out and practice fielding until your next turn to hit.

If he caught you loafing, he'd make a circular motion with his finger, and that meant you had to run and circle the ball park. A man that came to camp overweight had to run plenty of those laps around the field. Like Ike Boone. He was forty pounds over when he got there, and when he left, his suit hung on him like an overcoat.

Up to this time I had played right field for a number of years, but McGraw told me, "I don't know whether you'll play left field, center field or right field. You're a good sun fielder, and that may be the best thing you can do for me."

In the Polo Grounds the sun field was left field, and there he had Irish Meusel, who had come from Philadelphia to New York around the same time I did. Meusel was probably the best right-hand hitter in the league after Hornsby.

In right field McGraw had an amazing man, Ross Youngs, a very vicious player. He could hit line drives, run as fast as everything, slide straight into a bag and spring right up and go to the next base. He was a terrific right fielder and thrower, but he wasn't too good at playing the sun, so when right field was the sun field on the road McGraw generally would shift Youngs to center and put me in right.

But mostly in 1922 I alternated in center field with Bill Cunningham. I had the best year of my life at the bat. For half the season I was hitting .400, and I finished up at .368 for eighty-four games. In the World Series, in which the Giants beat the Yankees again, I was in two games and batted .400.

After the season there was a group of us that made an exhibition tour to the Far East. Herb Pennock was along— he was with the Red Sox then. From the Yankees we had Waite Hoyt, Freddy Hofmann and Joe Bush. We had George Kelly and Riggs Stephenson, Bib Falk and Amos Strunk.

George Moriarty, an American League umpire, went with us. And he was put in charge. They told him to supervise us on the field and as much as he could off the field. Judge Landis, the baseball commissioner, said he didn't want anybody to become bums on this trip. The ones who were married all took their wives. I wasn't married at the time, Hofmann wasn't married, George Kelly wasn't married.

We started on the *Empress of Canada* from Vancouver.

We played in Honolulu, and then went on and played all over Japan. Then we went over to China and Korea, and ended up playing in the Philippines.

In those days in Japan they didn't have big stadiums, but it was nothing for ten or twelve thousand people to come out to the games. They're pretty small, and they'd just squat along the sidelines and sit there. They were very interested in baseball. We played their universities and other teams. They wanted us to beat them as much as we could, so they could see the next time an American team came there if they were getting better.

On the way home we stopped at Hong Kong. There were people living out on the water in sampans, and a number of us bought chow dogs that the people were selling. The chow dogs then were not as red as they are now —they were more of a lion color. There were also some black ones.

We put them downstairs on the boat, where they had sort of a kennel section. First I had mine in a wicker cage on the deck, but when people came over to look at him he would get excited, because he'd never seen a group of strangers like that. And he was getting good and mad— he was sort of vicious like. So I put a tarpaulin over his cage, and finally I put him downstairs.

We got in a bad storm, and I was one of the few people that didn't get seasick, so I had to go down and feed all the dogs. In the dining room I'd say to the Chinese waiter, "I want fish and rice for bow-wow. Woof, woof, woof." And he'd get the idea.

Most of those dogs died on the way home, but I finally got mine back to Kansas City. We called him Ah Ming. My father became very attached to the dog. So did my brother, and so did my mother and my sister. Everybody in the neighborhood got to know Ah Ming, and he lived for about eight years.

I was the dog's favorite, the next one was my sister and the third one was my father. When I was away playing ball, my father used to take Ah Ming downtown every once in a while. He'd put the dog right up on a seat in a streetcar, and people would say, "What is that, mister?" They'd never seen any chow dogs around there. And my father would say, "That's a baby lion." And when they heard that, everybody would start scattering to seats further away in the car.

In 1923 spring training McGraw made me the same thing as manager of the second team. We always had two teams playing exhibition games. So with the B team going North, he called me over and said, "I'm taking an interest in you. Would you like to be a coach on this club in later days?"

I said, "Well, yes, I wouldn't mind being a coach."

He said, "I'll teach you all I can. Now we have Jimmy O'Connell in camp, we just paid seventy-five thousand dollars for him, and I'm going to keep him with the first team to see what he can do in center field. I know what you can do and what you can't do. So you go over and take that second team up North. I'm going to send Cozy Dolan with you."

O'Connell was a very good young player, but later on in 1924 he was thrown out of baseball, him and Cozy Dolan, for offering a bribe to Heinie Sand of the Phillies not to play hard against the Giants near the end of the pennant race.

Anyway, I went North with that second team. I'd had some experience at handling teams before—at Ole Miss and in the Navy and on barnstorming tours—but this was very good practice for me.

A lot of the men on the B team were put there as a sort of punishment. Earl Smith, a tough young catcher, was one. Evidently they searched our bags when we reported to camp, and they found a pair of handcuffs in Smith's luggage. Why Smith had the handcuffs, nobody knew. I guess some sheriff or somebody gave them to him. But McGraw didn't like it. He said to him, "Well, any fellow that reports with a pair of handcuffs—you can go with that second team."

If you think I didn't have any tact as a young ball-player, you should have seen Smith. He was a very fresh young man. It was nothing for him to squirt tobacco juice on the back of somebody that was walking past him at home plate. And if you were a coach, going back and forth to the lines, by the seventh inning you'd have a shower of tobacco spit all up the back of your uniform.

Toward the end of that trip North I began worrying about my job as a player, because O'Connell was starring in center field with the first team. So I wrote a letter that went something like, "Dear Mr. McGraw. It's very nice and wonderful of you to want to make me a coach later on in life, but I think it's time I came back and got in good shape so I can be ready to play for you—or ready to play for some other ball club if I am traded. So I think someone else can run this team better, and I would say Cozy Dolan. So I'm going to have Mr. Dolan run the team the rest of the way."

When I joined McGraw up at West Point, where the Giants always played an exhibition game before the start of the season, he asked me about some of the players on the B team. I said I didn't see why one of the pitchers had been sent back to the minors, as he had pitched pretty good ball. And I told him he should have kept Earl Smith, because Smith really did some great catching.

McGraw said, "Oh, you're going to tell me who to play now. You must be a pretty good manager. Now I'll give you a tip. How could you resign from managing that second team? You've been playing ball for a number of years. Did you ever sign a manager's contract?"

I said, "No, I didn't."

He said, "Well, how in the world could you fire yourself? That's another smart-aleck thing you did. Now I'll tell you what you'll do tonight. You'll stay out here at West Point after the game and tell those officers stories about the Giants." And he didn't leave anybody but Stengel there to talk to the officers.

I got him mad at me again in May of that year. Some friction had developed between me and a couple of men on the Philadelphia team. Now McGraw was very aggressive on the field, and he wanted you to be aggressive too, but he hated for you to get yourself thrown out of a game or suspended. Well, in this game these Philadelphia players kept telling their pitcher, Phil Weinert, that he should brush me off at the plate. And finally he hit me a good solid crack in the back.

So I went out to him with my bat and let the bat fly. Now when this bat flew, their whole team came out. They got me from behind and in front, and they really worked me over. One of them got a hold of my Adam's apple and squeezed it, and to this day I have about the largest Adam's apple you ever saw. For three days I couldn't eat, because to swallow hurt the Adam's apple going up and down.

I was thrown out of the game—there's a picture that's often been printed of some policemen leading me off the field. Mr. McGraw was mad because he was trying to rest Irish Meusel, who had a bad leg, and when I was put out of the game he had to put Meusel in.

He said to me, "That's the most asinine stunt I ever saw in my life." And "asinine" is one word I never forgot, whether I speak Stengelese or not. And he said, "If you're not suspended by the president of this league I'm going to suspend you myself." And it ended up that they both suspended me for a few days.

I got in trouble with McGraw another time that year. When we were on the road he'd have a trainer go around at night and check whether everybody was in their rooms on time. He'd knock on your door and call out your name, and you were supposed to answer. Sometimes players would pull tricks to fool the trainer, but McGraw would say, "If you people get this man fired, I'll hire another one. If he can't do the job I'll get one that will."

One night at the Auditorium Hotel in Chicago I was rooming with George McQuillan, a pitcher, and he sneaked out late. When the trainer got to our room I answered in two different voices for McQuillan and myself.

After McQuillan did get back he evidently became sick, and he forgot to clean it up in the morning. The maids reported it, and I got blamed for it. And when we came to leave town, Jesse Barnes and Earl Smith and myself were told that we'd been traded over to the Boston Braves. Judge Fuchs, the Boston owner, was right there at the station platform. He told Smitty he was going to give him a raise, he told Barnes he was going to give him a raise and he said the same thing to me.

I said, "You're not going to give me any raise. I'm staying on this ball club." And I got right on the train and found an empty berth and rode on to Pittsburgh.

The next day when I went out to the ball park, over came Dick Rudolph, who had pitched on the Braves and was now a coach on the team. He said, "We'll give you a thousand-dollar raise. We'll give you fifteen hundred. We'll give you two thousand. We'll give you three thousand. That's the last and biggest money you're going to get, and you'd better take it."

I said, "I'm not going to join you." And I went and saw Mr. McGraw and convinced him. So I didn't go to Boston then, although I did get traded there later on.

That 1923 season was another good hitting year for me. I played seventy-five games and batted .339. But about a month before the season ended I hurt my heel in Chicago. They had an iron fence over a concrete base. A long drive was hit into this fence, and I jumped in the air and came down on my heel on this concrete. A rivet that held my spikes on my shoes went up into my heel somewhat and gave me what was known as a stone bruise.

They finally got the swelling down, but this heel still hurt. When I touched there it would be just like a pinpoint. Before the World Series we worked out, and after each workout McGraw would call me over and say, "Is your heel well enough to play?" And I told him it wasn't.

Finally they thought of putting a soft red rubber pad in there to protect my heel. I taped it to my shoe on the inside. I thought it would hold, although baseball shoes in those days were cut real low, so you could glide faster when you were running.

Well, we came up to the last inning of the first game, which was played at Yankee Stadium, and the score was

4-4. The fielding had been amazing. I would say that the game was actually won for us on amazing plays by Frank Frisch and George Kelly.

One play came after Babe Ruth had hit a triple for the Yankees with one out. Bob Meusel then hit a ball out to center field. I was playing too deep to get it, but Frisch turned around from second and came out and made an almost impossible catch. And when he caught the ball he jumped in the air and spun right around, and threw the ball to home plate. It was a perfect throw, and they tagged Ruth out trying to score after the catch.

Another play was when Joe Dugan was on third base with one out and Ruth was at bat. People won't believe this now, but Ruth at this time was choking up on the bat about three inches, because we'd been throwing him so many bad pitches. He went up there just to meet the ball with a man on third, and he sent a terrific drive down the first-base line. I don't know how George Kelly stopped it, but he made a leaping stop of the ball and picked it up and threw out Dugan at home.

The most amazing part of it was that Kelly was playing back. With Ruth at the plate, he wasn't playing in to try to cut off the run. So Dugan thought he could surely score. But Ruth hit a bullet, and Kelly just got Dugan at the plate with that wonderful arm of his.

So that helped us to stay even with them through eight innings. In the ninth I hit this line drive out to left center between Whitey Witt and Bob Meusel. As I was making the turn at second base I had the feeling that this shoe with the heel pad was going to come off. So I commenced dragging the shoe, and everybody said afterward that I looked like an old man out there. McGraw said, "Why, he was running on one leg."

But I kept on coming. Whitey Witt, the center fielder, picked up the ball and relayed it to Bob Meusel, the left fielder, who had the strongest arm in baseball at that time. As I was just about to round third base I could see who had that ball, but I kept on going.

Mr. Meusel let that ball fly. Near the end I could tell I was going to be safe, because that throw was just a fraction off line from home plate. I saw that the catcher, Wally Schang, wasn't going to be able to get it unless he moved two feet away from the plate, which stopped him from giving me a good block before he caught the ball. And I slid in there before he could wheel back around and tag me out.

Nobody had expected me to be a hero in that World Series, and rightly so. Everybody picked Frisch, Ross Youngs, Irish Meusel, George Kelly and Dave Bancroft to be the stars of our club, along with Heinie Groh.

When I got that inside-the-park homer, it was on a change-up thrown by Joe Bush. Miller Huggins, the Yankee manager, wouldn't believe it. He said to his players—he didn't say it to the newspapermen—"I used to play and manage against Stengel in the National League, and I know that you pull the string on him." That means a change-up.

Then in the third game, when I won a 1-0 pitching duel for Art Nehf with a home run in the seventh inning off the original Sad Sam Jones, he also threw me a change-up. I hit it into the right-field stands. That's the time I put my thumb to my nose as I circled the bases, and got reprimanded for it by Judge Landis.

I wound up hitting .417 for the Series. But the Yankees came back and beat us in the Series for the first time. And a month later Mr. McGraw traded Dave Bancroft, Bill Cunningham and myself to Boston.

Although I was still only thirty-three years old, it was beginning to look as though I didn't have too much longer to go as a big-league ballplayer. But there were other things I could look forward to. I had met the girl I wanted to marry, and I thought that after I finished playing, I could go on and support her by becoming a manager.

12

✂ Some ballplayers, when they get a chance at managing will copy after another manager. That's a very serious mistake. You can take some of a man's methods, but don't ever think you can imitate him. You have to be yourself.

Would you try to copy Connie Mack, who won ten pennants with the old Philadelphia Athletics? He was an amazing manager. I met this lovely man, and when I became a minor-league manager I sold him players and conversed with him, and watched World Series games in which he was the manager. And every player of his I talked to said, "Why, we never played for a man that nice." But some of these people weren't that nice themselves, and they couldn't manage by his methods.

The greatest manager I played for was John McGraw, and when I started managing, everybody said, "I'll bet he's going to copy McGraw." Well, there's been anywhere from fifteen to fifty men that tried to imitate McGraw and never made it, because he was an amazing man as well as manager, and he had his own way about him.

He was strict about everything—probably stricter than any manager could be with ballplayers today. He was the first manager I saw who even watched your diet. He went over the players' meal checks in the hotels to see whether they were eating the right kind of meals.

With no night baseball then, he always wanted you in bed by twelve o'clock at night, and he also wanted you out at the ball park by ten or ten-thirty in the morning. If you were starring, the way Frank Frisch generally was in my time, you could be excused from taking the early workout and come back later. But you had to check in first at ten or ten-thirty unless you'd arranged in advance to go to the dentist or something like that.

There was no question about any of this with McGraw. If you didn't do it he took some of your money. In the old days they'd fine you but make you play. They couldn't fine a man over ten days' pay unless it went to the president of the league. But they could fine you as much as nine days' pay and make you play the nine days.

Or McGraw would trade you, because he always figured, "I can buy you back if you're any good." He didn't carry hatred. If a man had been gone two years, he never said, "I'd like to get that guy back, but he don't like me and I don't like him." If the man could help the club win, he got him.

Maybe some of my players didn't like me either, but it wasn't because I was that strict. I very seldom fined a man. In my last few years with the Yankees, I didn't have a finger in a single fine that was made on that club. I sometimes threatened players that they were going to run into fines or be traded. But I never did fine a man a tremendous sum. With some of them I could see it was useless, and anyway, rather than take a man's money during the season, I'd rather give him until the end of the year and then say, "Well, I can't go to bat with the front office for you on your salary"—assuming that I could do it for some men.

In spring training in 1956 we had quite a bit of friction in the Yankee camp about one of our pitchers, Don Larsen, and whether his habits were okay. This was a man that liked to drink beer, liked to sit up. He could go any place very proper, never got in fights or disputes, but he did not know the hours of baseball. Sometimes he would get mixed up on when it was time to go home.

He ran his automobile into a tree late one night there in Florida, and I was told that if I didn't do something desperate to Mr. Larsen it would kill the morale of the club. But with a group of men who are of age and have families, I doubt that if one man does something one night, the other twenty-four would feel they had to go out and do the same thing. So I stuck with Mr. Larsen, after telling him that it would cost him a lot of money if he got into any more trouble, and that his job with the club was at stake. And after I stuck with him I commenced getting the payoff. He won eleven and lost only five for us during the season, and of course you know what he did for us in the World Series, pitching that perfect game against Brooklyn.

McGraw probably would have handled the situation some other way, and his way probably would have worked too. Some men didn't play good for McGraw—at least they said they didn't. They'd say, "Why, this man's never satisfied with me." I thought that McGraw did great with me, because I had to run out every ball, I had to play good. And if I didn't play good, he thought that there was something wrong with me or that I wasn't putting out enough. I thought I was hustling all the time, but he'd see where I could have put out a little extra.

McGraw wanted every play executed properly, and if you couldn't do it after he'd told you two or three times, he figured you were either too stupid or too awkward to play for him.

Against the Cardinals once I had to chase a ball to deep center field. I picked it up and threw it in low to George Kelly, the first baseman, who had such a wonderful arm that he went out as relay man on extra base hits. There was no need for him to stay and cover first if the batter was going for extra bases.

Well, Kelly had to lean down and get my throw on the short pickup, and then he had to hop, skip, jump, and throw it. The base runner, Hornsby, who was one of the fastest men in the league then, was called safe at home by an inch, and that run beat us.

McGraw said to me after the game, "From now on, young man, be sure you look at that relay man and throw the ball up high at his head or shoulders, where he can throw it home without taking a hop, skip and jump. You lost that game for me. And if you don't do better you will be back with those tail-end bums in Philadelphia." So after that I remembered to throw the ball high.

Just let you get into a bad streak, and he'd call you over and say, "Now this isn't any news to me. I knew you were going to become a bum and start being careless. You're just egotistical, and you're just trying to get some base hits. You're not thinking and keeping your mind on the game. When a man makes an error you don't even know where the runners are or where to throw the ball."

He wanted you to be a fighter at the plate and not give in to the pitcher, whatever happened. Stand in there, don't back off an inch, and get a piece of the ball. Something may happen.

He also was very alert on when to start the runners, when to start double steals, and he was very good on not having you caught off a base. He hated to see you just walk off a base sluggishly. He said the first two steps off a base, if the batter hit the ball, might make you be safe at third or safe at home plate.

But after the lively ball came in he knew that he had to cut down on the base-running and go to slugging. He was the best manager I ever saw at adapting from the dead ball to the lively ball. At the plate he'd let you go for the slug on three and nothing, two and nothing, three and one—if there were men on bases. If there weren't men on bases he'd get very disturbed at you if you didn't stand up there and fight the pitcher, especially with two strikes.

One day I took a third strike—the man curved the ball, and I was asleep at the plate. After I came into the bench, he said, "Why didn't you hit that last pitch? That wasn't far from the plate. Chances are it was over the plate—that's a pretty good umpire. Were you guessing? Why weren't you ready up there to fight on that pitch and get a piece of it before it got to the catcher's glove?"

And I said, "Well, I thought—"

And he said, "Don't think for me. Act!"

McGraw liked to call most of the signs for the pitchers, unless he had a very experienced catcher. Every time he had a pitcher that had control and could get ahead in the count, McGraw generally could mix the hitters up a lot. In the seventh, eighth and ninth innings he'd call many a breaking ball. As soon as the lively ball came in, he figured that the fast ball could be hit too far in the outfield. He wanted grounders to be hit, like Paul Richards and Al Lopez do at the present time. And as the hitters began swinging harder, going for home runs, they chased more bad pitches. And that's when McGraw went to change-ups—to pitching slow balls to get the hitter off stride.

Offensively he was a terrific manager—and defensively too. But offensively, he would try to get in the lead straight off. If you got three or four runs ahead of him at the start of a game that would drive him crazy, because then all he could do was try and catch up. He couldn't maneuver as much.

John McGraw was one of the three best managers in all the years I played in the National League—him and Frank Chance of the Cubs and Fred Clarke of Pittsburgh. I learned more from McGraw than anybody. But every manager I played for on the way up had some outstanding points.

My first manager in the big leagues, Bill Dahlen at Brooklyn, was good with pitchers, and as I mentioned earlier, he was very good on sliding. He said, "You can't slide good." And I thought I could, but he showed me I had to improve.

The next one was Wilbert Robinson. Uncle Robbie was very jolly, and wonderful to work for. He would make you think he thought you were better than you were.

He would take me out of the line-up against the good left-handed pitchers, but he did it with tact. If he put Jimmy Johnston in there and Johnston didn't get a hit, Robbie would call me over the next day and say, "Gee, I couldn't sleep last night. I made such a terrible mistake not putting you in that ball game." And if it happened another time, he'd say, "I made that mistake again."

Now he hadn't made any mistake and he knew it. He just liked to keep you feeling good.

Robbie loved old players—men that were experienced. He loved to get an old pitcher that had a bad arm, because he knew the man was brighter than when he was young and could throw harder. He took Rube Marquard and Larry Cheney and several others that were supposed to be over the hill and made exceptional pitchers out of them, because he showed them how to take advantage of their experience.

And in later years with the Yankees I'd often pick up an old pitcher during the pennant race, like John Sain and Sal Maglie and Jim Konstanty. I'd get the old man to fool the youth of America. You have the old man go two or three innings in relief, and the young ballplayers can't hit him. He's too slick for them. He gets them off stride and makes them hit at a bad pitch.

So I followed Robbie's example there. But he hated a little pitcher, which I don't go along with. Robinson had no confidence in a little pitcher against a big hitter. He liked pitchers that were over six feet tall, like the basketball players today. He used to get so mad when a little pitcher beat him, like Dick Rudolph of the Braves.

And Robbie just couldn't stand a weak hitter on his club, no matter what else the man could do. He couldn't sit on the bench and manage and see a weak hitter go up there three or four times. Now a good hitter—he could stand for the fellow being club-footed, and stumbling and falling down. Robbie could overlook some of that if the fellow could hit the ball hard. So managers can have weak points too.

At Pittsburgh my manager was Hugo Bezdek. They put him there in wartime. He never played big-league ball, but he was experienced in sports—he was the football coach for many years at Penn State. He'd been good at basketball, and he knew something about baseball. And Mr. Dreyfuss, the Pittsburgh owner, told him, "This is an experienced ball club. Handle it for a while, and then I'll put in another manager if I see fit."

The best thing Bezdek taught me was that if you have any doubt about how a play should be made, you should find out about it. So Bezdek would hold meetings and ask questions of the experienced players on the club. He'd ask Vic Saier, who had come from the Cubs, how Frank Chance did certain things there. He'd ask Billy Hinchman, a good hitter, what percentages he followed in place-hitting and slugging. He'd ask Max Carey, a great base runner, what was the best system for running bases. He'd ask his questions about something at a meeting, and then he'd decide, "This is the way we're going to do it here."

At Philadelphia I played under Gavvy Cravath first, and he was good at teaching hitting, but he didn't have much of a pitching staff. Then Bill Donovan came in. I wouldn't say that on some things—the infielding—he was as good as other managers. But he'd been a pitcher, and he was wonderful with pitchers.

He'd say to a man, "How can you keep making the same mistakes? I was wild when I started out too. But you don't do anything about it. You don't work enough."

Or he'd say, "Do you know why I can't keep you in a game nine innings? You've made up your mind in three innings that this just ain't your day. You've got it in your mind that you can only pitch on certain days."

And I found out as a manager that some pitchers, with no alibi at all, will get it into their mind that it isn't their day and get off the beam. They get wild. They do everything wrong.

When I got my first chance to do some managing in 1925 it was very important for me to make good, as I'd become a married man the year before. I met my wife Edna through my Philadelphia and New York teammate, Irish Meusel. Edna and Irish's wife had both come originally from the same town, Menominee, Michigan. Edna's family, the Lawsons, later moved to Glendale, California, and she eventually went to work for Howard Byron. He was the tax collector for the city of Los Angeles, and believe me, he's collected many a tax.

Mrs. Stengel can tell the whole story much better than I can, and you should ask her about it.

13

(*Mrs. Stengel Now Speaking*)

✂ Our meeting each other came about by accident. I was planning on spending my 1923 vacation up in Portland, Oregon. And my friend Van Meusel, who was Mrs. Irish Meusel, persuaded me to come to New York instead, saying that it could possibly be Irish's last year with the Giants. And if I wanted to see New York, he had contacts to get choice seats in all the theaters and all the night spots. And there was also major-league baseball. But that was no selling point to me then—the baseball part. So my family approved my going. After all, I could go to Portland, Oregon, any time.

A boy friend I had in Glendale, Perry Smith, said, "I'll lend you my trunk if you want to go to New York City." So I borrowed Perry Smith's trunk.

I was working in the Hall of Records in Los Angeles at the time. I was in the budget department under Howard Byron, who became the treasurer and tax collector. He just retired a short time ago.

So I approached him for a six-week to two-month leave of absence, which he didn't approve of too much. But he finally said, "Well, as long as you're going to see major-league baseball"—he was quite a baseball fan, and he consented. So my vacation started in the middle of July, and I was due back around the first of September.

I first went to Atlantic City. I was met in Philadelphia by Mrs. Meusel and Mrs. Ethel Chambers, who worked in Philadelphia. And they took me to her home in Atlantic City, and we enjoyed swimming and walking on the boardwalk. Jimmy O'Connell's wife was down there at the same time, and Bob Meusel's wife, Edith, was there also.

So we had quite a house party. And most of the conversation was that they wanted me to meet a very eligible bachelor on the club by the name of Casey Stengel, who was a lot of fun and was considered a very good dancer and a big spender. Of course, all these qualifications were along the line that anyone would be seeking who was taking a vacation.

After a week in Atlantic City we went to New York, and Irish Meusel came in from a road trip that night. The next day we went to the ball park and sat in a box to the right of the dugout. And the girls pointed out, "There's Casey over there in center field." I didn't know where center field was, but I saw somebody out there.

I didn't follow the game too closely, but pretty soon I saw this man in center field going into the dugout, and I guess I asked, "Did he get hurt?" The girls were reluctant to tell me, but I found out later that the Giants were replacing Casey and putting Jimmy O'Connell out there because he could cover more ground. They were using Casey mostly for his hitting and Jimmy for the fielding.

When the game was over we waited for the men to get dressed, and finally we started toward the runway. And up the runway came Casey Stengel, wearing a very attractive brown-and-black checked suit. He had a straw hat on his head, and incidentally, he always did wear hats pretty well.

Of course the girls introduced me, and finally the other men showed up. And Casey said, "Can I walk over to the apartment with you?" Then he wanted to know if he couldn't take us all out to dinner and dancing that night. Unfortunately I already had a date with a doctor from Brooklyn, so he said, "Well, how about tomorrow night?"

So that was our first date. I might add that on our first date we were never alone a minute, and it was that way the whole six or seven days I was in New York. One night Casey took us all to the movies, and I have a faint recollection that he might have held my hand during the show.

When I left we said good-bye, with all the girls and their husbands around, but he did make a date to meet me on the road in Chicago, where I was going to stop on my way back and visit the Hartnetts, who were friends of my family. So Casey came out there on an off day, and I will say that Mrs. Hartnett was much more co-operative than the Meusels, who had arranged for me to meet Casey in New York and then never left us alone for one minute. Mrs. Hartnett stayed upstairs and the maid was in the kitchen. Casey put the Victrola on and we danced. And Mrs. Hartnett said afterward the one mistake we made was that Casey didn't change the record all afternoon.

That night we went out to dinner and dancing, and taking me back in a cab, Casey mentioned that his time was limited, that he must be back in the team's hotel not

later than twelve o'clock. I think it was because of the
rush deal that Casey proposed to me on Mrs. Hartnett's
front porch that evening.

I didn't pledge myself to accept, but we corresponded.
I sent my picture to him, and he said the picture sold his
folks in Kansas City. And for Christmas—he probably
wanted more letters, because the first gift he gave me was
a solid-gold fountain pen.

The next year Casey was with the Boston Braves, and
he kept wanting to know when I was coming East again.
And he asked for the address of my brother, Larry Lawson, an Army officer stationed in Belleville, Illinois, which
is outside St. Louis. Little did I know that Casey was
going to ask my brother to intercede to get me to set a
wedding date.

He called on my brother and his wife when the Braves
were in St. Louis, and he made quite an impression on
them. They persuaded me to come visit them that summer
at a time when Casey would be in town.

I told Howard Byron at the office in Los Angeles that I
would only be gone a couple of weeks this time. He said,
"Are you sure you're not going to get married?" And I
said, "No, sir. I'm positive."

Well, Casey got permission to go to St. Louis a couple
of days ahead of his team, and that gave him about
five days. Things were very convenient in Belleville. My
brother was on duty from five in the morning until noon,
and my sister-in-law used to go off and have coffee with
the other wives. So that was the first time we were really
alone for any length of time.

We talked things over quite a bit. On his last night in
town—well, I guess Casey had just made up his mind that
he wasn't going to leave St. Louis without me. So we

made up our minds that we would be married the next day.

Casey had to get permission from his manager, Dave Bancroft. We called on Dave in his hotel room, and Casey said, "Dave, I want to get married tomorrow. Could I have an extra day off and meet you in Chicago?" And Dave was all for it.

My brother made the arrangements. We were to pick up the marriage license at the city hall the next morning, and a Catholic priest, Father Louis Ell, was to marry us at two o'clock in the afternoon.

Casey had hoped we could go through the city hall without being noticed, but when my brother went down the corridor, all you could hear were his Army spurs—clinkety, clank, clank. And people would look out of offices, and apparently they were buzzing and saying, "That looks like Casey Stengel."

The only chapel in town was in the local hospital. Father Ell was going to marry us there, but he asked my brother, "Say, that wouldn't by any chance be Casey Stengel, the ballplayer, would it?" And my brother said yes. Father Ell said, "Oh, my, my. We can't have this marriage performed in the hospital. I'll get permission from the bishop to hold it in his residence."

So on August 18, 1924, Father Ell—who later became a bishop himself—married us in the parlor of Bishop Henry Althoff's residence. Immediately after the wedding we went back to my brother's home and got busy sending telegrams to our folks. But before we got the telegrams out, the families had already been notified by the newspapers—the news went out over the Associated Press.

We had our wedding dinner on the roof of the Chase Hotel in St. Louis that night, and took a midnight train

and arrived in Chicago the next morning. We had break-
fast in the dining room of the team's hotel. Though I didn't
notice it, I guess Casey was taking a lot of kidding from
all the ballplayers that morning.

That afternoon Casey pretty well starred. As I recall, it
was a doubleheader. Casey got two hits—one was a home
run, and the other, I'm pretty sure, was a hit that won one
of the games.

Then the team went to Pittsburgh, and from there to
New York. We had quite a gathering there—Irish and
Van Meusel, Bob and Edith Meusel, the Herb Pennocks
and the Aaron Wards. They invited Casey and myself to
go out to dinner. I guess Casey had entertained all those
wives on his trip to Japan in 1922, and now they wanted
to entertain us.

We went out to a restaurant called Hunter's Inn, I
believe. Babe Ruth was also there with a group. We had
quite a nice evening of dancing and all. And when the
evening was over, Casey caught the bill for both Babe
Ruth's group and our own.

Earlier in the year Casey had been invited by John
McGraw to go on a post-season exhibition tour to Eng-
land with the New York Giants and the Chicago White
Sox. So that became our honeymoon trip. There were
three other newly married couples on board—Walter
Huntzinger and his wife, Ross Youngs and his wife and
Mr. and Mrs. Miller. Mrs Miller was a secretary in the
Giants' office.

We had a beautiful trip going over to England, where
we landed at Liverpool. From there we went to Ireland,
where the boys were supposed to play a game, but it
rained the whole time. Then we went to London for ten

days, and the food wasn't too good, but we did have an awful lot of fun.

When they played a game before the King and Queen, I don't think I was too impressed. I wound up having tea with Queen Mary, but if there'd been any better place to go that day, I'd probably have gone there instead.

Prior to the game the boys pantomimed baseball in slow motion, and I enjoyed that more than I had any regular ball game up to then. My eye was caught by a fellow at first base. I thought he was very funny, and I asked Blanche McGraw, who was sitting next to me, which player that was.

She said, "Don't you know your own husband?" Of course, the seats were pretty far back from the field, and then I was used to seeing Casey play center field, not first base.

From London we went to Paris, and that was the best part of the whole trip—the shops and the well-dressed people and the food. Every night was New Year's Eve. Paris in 1924 was certainly not the same city I returned to in 1954. In 1924 they were glad to wait on you in the stores, which was a great deal different from the way it is today in any part of Europe.

Coming back we were on the *Leviathan*. It was the greatest boat afloat at the time, and we had luxurious accommodations. And the trip lasted seven days, and at the end of it the steward said to Casey, "Well, your wife was the sickest one on the boat but never missed a meal."

After we got back to New York the McGraws persuaded us to stay on for a week. Then we spent six weeks with Casey's folks in Kansas City, and then we came out to Glendale to see my folks. They were building this home for us—my father was a big builder and real-estate man in Glendale, just as he had been previously in Michigan. We moved into the house one week after we arrived, and it has been our home ever since.

I must say Casey should have had a shot in the arm before he stepped off the train the day we got out there, because of what he had facing him when he came out of that station. There was my mother and my father; my sister and her husband and their two very tiny children, and my brother Jack, who was then in his first year in college. And when Casey looked up and saw that array of people—well, he didn't pull at my skirt, but he certainly was looking for me to take him by the hand and lead him right into the family group.

But I know he wasn't around very long before he realized that he was more than welcome. And it's been a very, very close relationship—not only those he met at the time, but the second generation that has followed.

(*Back to Casey*)

✂ After the wedding I told the writers, "If you're going to print anything about us, you can say for the bridegroom that it is the best catch he ever made in his career."

And we never had any children, but Edna had so many in her family—nieces and nephews and their children that came along—that we became very active with the family. We'd have big Sundays in which our home in Glendale became a playground for the kids.

And as I progressed in baseball as a manager, Edna got to where she was very enthusiastic, liked most of the owners and commenced taking an interest in the game. She was a good dresser, and I thought she made a good appearance in any box wherever I had a position as a manager.

And I've gone along with this one number, and I would have to say that her end of things has been handled in a first-class manner, with me being a man that's been up and down.

14

✂️ Well, at the time I got married in 1924 my big-league playing days were coming to an end. I finished out the season with the Boston Braves—I hit .280 that year in 131 games—and I started the 1925 season with them too. Then in May the Boston owner, Judge Fuchs, decided to buy a farm club at Worcester in the Eastern League, and he sent me there to run it. I was the president and the manager, and also a player.

Edna didn't like it very much at first in this small league. But she began to enjoy herself more when Judge Fuchs got the team a bus—one of the first that was ever put in baseball. I'd take her with us on those bus trips through the hills of New England and down to Albany, New York. She loved the beautiful scenery and the winding little roads.

I'd stand in the front of the bus and hold team meetings. I'd talk to each player and ask him about the plays of the game, and what he thought about the team we were playing tomorrow. And we'd go over how to pitch to the different men on their team, and how to bat against their pitchers.

Shanty Hogan was at Worcester that year—a great big

catcher with a tremendous appetite. On these bus trips he'd keep putting up his hand for us to stop. He always wanted the bus to pull up whenever he saw a restaurant.

The Worcester club was in last place when I came there on May twentieth. The previous manager, Eddie Eayrs, was supposed to be discharged, but I had them keep him on the team as a player. He led the club in hitting and helped get us up to third place in the final standings.

One of the other clubs in the league was New Haven. George Weiss was running the team and owned it. He'd gone to Yale. He was doing very good in selling ballplayers, and when he sold one he'd sometimes take Mrs. Stengel and myself out to help him celebrate.

I kept acquainted with George Weiss over the years. I'd see him at the different baseball meetings. He went with the Yankees, and eventually was put in charge of their office. And he used his influence later on to see if he couldn't get me to become the Yankee manager.

Another man in the league was Leo Durocher. He was a young shortstop at Hartford. He couldn't hit much, but he certainly could get around and get that ball and take relays. He was a great fielder, and a sharp man and quick-witted.

We used to get mad at him all the time, and we'd have one fight after another. One day when I got to the ball park early before a Hartford game they were holding a meeting in their clubhouse. Durocher wasn't hitting but about .208 at the time. And I went out to the shortstop position and scratched "208" in the dirt in figures about six feet long. And you ought to have seen his face when he came out and saw that. Of course, he knew then that I was a big smart aleck, the same as himself.

But it didn't faze him at all. You never could get Durocher's nerve. We might even have won the pennant that year if he hadn't thrown some of my men out at home on relays—and with me coaching at third and sending them in myself.

After my year at Worcester I thought I'd fulfilled my obligation to the Braves. I was a ten-year man in the big leagues and entitled to be a free agent as a player, but they were using me for other positions. So I released myself. I wrote a letter releasing "Charles D. Stengel, Manager," signed by "Charles D. Stengel, President."

Judge Fuchs, the owner, didn't like that very much. But the commissioner of baseball, Judge Landis, looked it over and said, "Well, I guess if he's president of the club and could hire and fire players, he can also fire himself as manager."

The next year, 1926, I got a job managing in the highest classification of the minor leagues at Toledo in the American Association. One of my owners there, Oscar Smith, wrote me a little while ago on how that came about.

John McMahon and I were partners in Toledo in the practice of law, and we were also interested in real estate. We arrived at the conclusion that the location of the old Swayne Field baseball park would improve and could some day be developed. John McGraw of the Giants, who owned the park and the Toledo team, said that they would not sell the property unless we also bought the ball club. Of course, neither John McMahon nor I knew anything about baseball, let alone trying to run a club. We told this to McGraw, and McGraw said, "I can recommend the best man I think for you in the operation of the ball club who can handle and develop players, manage the club properly and in addition has business ability. He will produce a successful operation for you and one that will appeal to the public."

It was Casey Stengel whom he recommended. Everything that McGraw said came true. Through Casey's efforts the ball club became a city project and had the endorsement of the whole community. Attendance grew so that in 1927 we played to 324,000 people, which was more than the population, and we won the first pennant in Toledo's history.

The rivalry was very great in that league. All the clubs fought with each other. It was nothing for one guy to have a black eye one day, and another one the next day, and so on and so forth. And when you got in trouble they would suspend you. This happened to me after a couple of fights, which my owners didn't like, and which was a lesson to me about better use of tact on the ball field.

I also got into too much trouble with umpires—he'd push me and I'd push him. And Judge Landis told me, "From here on you'd better have gloves on when you touch an umpire, or I'm going to suspend you a full year."

Managing in the minor leagues was different in those days, before the major-league farm systems took over. Toledo was an independent team. So I had to become a salesman. I had to become a publicity man. I had to talk to writers. I had to develop my players. I had to do it with words, and by working with them with the fungo bat on the ball field.

You also were supposed to win, but if you couldn't win, then you had to make assets out of enough players so you could sell them. You generally needed to sell four or five men a season for the club to get by financially.

I had authority to hire, fire and sell any players. My salary was $10,000, and I had an unlimited expense account to entertain big-league scouts that came in to look over our men. If a player didn't look good the first day a scout saw him, I'd persuade the scout to stay over. I'd keep him there a week. I never got a commission when we sold a player, so even if the man didn't make good, the scouts knew I hadn't pushed the sale just to make money for myself.

I sold men like Freddy Maguire and Woody English to the Cubs, and Roy Parmalee to the Giants. And Bevo Le-Bourveau—I kept selling him and getting him back. I sold him to John McGraw in New York and Connie Mack in Philadelphia and Branch Rickey in St. Louis—three of the brightest men that ever were in baseball.

LeBourveau was an unfortunate player. He could do more than almost anybody else, as I'd found out a few years before when we both were on the Phillies, and he was sensational on the bases. But he was very erratic, and he was a nervous Frenchman. He'd get in arguments that got so strong that he couldn't stay with the teams he went to.

But at Toledo he was one of my meal tickets—Le-Bourveau and Bobby Veach. Veach had started out with me at Kankakee and became a terrific hitter at Detroit with Ty Cobb and Sam Crawford. He had been let out in the majors, so I got him to sign up at Toledo.

I said, "You live in Detroit. Why don't you come down on that highway and play for me, and I'll let you go home every night." We had no night ball then in Toledo, so he could drive home to Detroit after every game, and then come down again the next day.

I got other men down from the big leagues, like Jack Scott, Rosy Ryan, Walter Huntzinger, Johnny Neun. All but Neun had been with me on the Giants—Mr. McGraw gave me a lot of advice and help on getting players. At Toledo I kept blending these older men in with the kids.

You might say I was already platooning, which I became known for later on.

I remember one day when I possibly did too much of it. We were playing at home and getting beat by a run, and we filled the bases with two out in the ninth inning. Our catcher was coming up to bat, but I thought I could do a better job against this right-handed pitcher, Lynn Nelson, so I said, "I'm going to hit for the catcher."

That happened to be the second catcher I'd used in the game, and some of my players tried to stop me from going up there. They said, "Don't you know you haven't got another catcher?"

I knew that, all right. My idea was that it didn't make any difference, because if I got a hit we'd win the game and if I didn't we'd lose it. Either way the game was over.

So what does that pitcher do but walk me? That ties the score. Our next hitter goes out. Now we have to go into extra innings, and I don't have any catcher. But I was fortunate. Walter Huntzinger, a pitcher, volunteered to catch. He said he used to catch at times in high school.

Naturally the other team figured they could run wild on the bases against Huntzinger. But he never had to throw. Jack Scott, who was pitching for us, didn't allow a man to get on base, and we finally won the game in ten or eleven innings.

I've tried that three or four times in my managing career and won. The only time I got good and caught with it was with the Yankees later on, when I had to put Hank Bauer in to catch, and a passed ball went by him to beat us.

Another Toledo story that's often been told is about the days when everybody was playing the stock market. This was before the big market crash. The Toledo club had slipped, and I noticed that when our guys were reading newspapers in the clubhouse, they always seemed to be on the stock sheet instead of the sports page.

So this day I was holding a meeting, and I went over the team we were going to play—their weaknesses and so forth. And some of the guys, instead of listening to me, were still looking at that stock page.

Finally I said, "Now I'm going to give you a tip. Do you know that I don't think you're paying any attention to baseball? Every time I come in here, you're on the stock sheet. And I'm going to give you a tip on the market. I'd advise you to buy Sante Fe railroad stock." And some of them asked why, and I said, "This next month they are going to be doing the biggest business they ever had, because a whole lot of you fellows are going to be riding out of here on those trains."

I only had one-year contracts in my six years at Toledo, but the owners would always rehire me, although we had our ups and downs in the standings, since we kept selling off good players.

After we won the pennant in 1927 the owners used the profits to expand the ball park from 4,500 to 14,000 grandstand seats. To rebuild a ball park during the winter is a very costly operation. And the owners didn't know the depression was coming, and the club became very indebted to the banks.

Then in 1931 five of the six banks in which we had our money closed down. We had just deposited checks which had come in for the sale of ballplayers, and that money was frozen too. I also lost a lot of my personal money. It ended up that we were out of baseball, and the franchise was taken over by the Cleveland ball club.

Commissioner Landis, being a strict old man, wanted to be sure that everything at Toledo was on the up and up. He sent Leslie O'Connor to examine our books, and found that the bank closings had made it almost impossible to keep them straight.

Then he called me to go see him in Chicago, and he said, "I have a method of bringing in a ballplayer or an owner, and when I look them straight in the face and they look me straight in the face, they generally tell me the truth."

I explained the things that had gone wrong, and I told him that the ballplayers had all received their salaries in full for the season. And he kept asking me, "Are you sure you didn't take any commissions on the sales of players?"

I said, "No, sir, I did not." And finally I said, "If you want to add this to the list of debts the club owes, here's a couple of personal notes for money I advanced myself."

Judge Landis looked at them, and then he said, "Young man, don't you know some other good, safe business you could get into, like shoveling manure?"

Over the winter Max Carey, who was managing at Brooklyn, gave me an opportunity to be a coach under him. I'd played with Max at Pittsburgh. He was the best base stealer I ever saw—he once stole fifty-one bases in fifty-three attempts—and they have him now in the Hall of Fame.

I appreciated his offer very much. The job paid $7000, which was the least I'd made in baseball from the time I got married in 1924, but it was a lot more money than most people were getting in those depression times.

Brooklyn finished third under Carey in 1932, then the next year the club didn't do so well. I was surprised people didn't realize Carey had a club that was getting near the end of its age—you could just see it was dropping off. But in February of 1934 they called me to New York City and told me they'd decided to make a change, and offered me the managing job.

I said, "Well, I understand he's got another year on his contract."

They said, "That's what he has. Max Carey had a contract for another year."

I said, "Well, does he get his money or doesn't he?"

They said, "That's not for you to worry about. We'll give you the information that if you don't take this job, there are fifty others that will."

15

✄   Well, I took the Brooklyn managing job when it was offered to me in February of '34. I couldn't see that I'd be helping Max Carey any by not taking it. And I'm glad to say that Carey eventually did get paid the money that was coming to him for that year.

One of the nicest messages of congratulations I got after signing up was from my old Brooklyn manager, Wilbert Robinson, who had become president of the Atlanta ball club. Robbie wrote me, "I am sure pleased you have the position as manager of the Brooklyn Club. I know you will do well, in fact better than anyone I know of, with the material you have."

The big thing in New York City then was the rivalry between the Dodgers and the Giants. With the five-cent subway fare, you could go over to Ebbets Field in Brooklyn for a nickel, and you could come back and go over to the Polo Grounds in New York for a nickel. You could get big crowds in either park when the two clubs played, because the local people of New York and the local people of Brooklyn would go out to root against each other.

The situation got coked up even more my first year as Brooklyn manager because of a remark by Bill Terry, who was doing very splendidly as manager of the Giants. He was talking to some writers before the season about the chances of the different teams in the pennant race, and Roscoe McGowan of the *New York Times* asked him, "What about Brooklyn?"

And Terry made the mistake of joking. He said, "Why, are they still in the league?"

Well, that caused quite a bit of feeling over in Brooklyn, naturally. But during the season the Giants went ahead and beat us almost every series. They were in first place most of the year, then in September the St. Louis Cardinals began to catch up to them. One reason was that the Cardinals got special permission to make up a couple of rained-out games with us in a doubleheader, which the Dean brothers won for them. Terry could have protested and kept those games from being played, but he didn't, and he never got the credit for this that he deserved.

Anyhow, going into the last two days of the season the Giants and Cardinals were tied for first place. The Cardinals had two games with Cincinnati, which they won, while we played the Giants twice in the Polo Grounds.

It was mostly Brooklyn people that filled the stands for those games. They bought banners, and they'd march up and down the aisles every time we'd make a run or two. That kept going on all the way through, because in the first game we beat the Giants, 5-1, behind our big pitcher, Van Mungo, and in the second game we beat them, 8-5.

I remember that Tony Cuccinello, our second baseman, had a very good hitting series. In the last game there were two times when they thought he was going to bunt and he swung and bounced the ball over third base and down into the left-field corner. Once he got a double and the other time a triple.

Those were a couple of sad days for the Giants. Bill Terry said later it was a good thing I didn't come over to his clubhouse to shake hands with him after the last game, because the Giants would have kicked me right back into my own clubhouse.

When we got dressed and went outside, the jams of people were enormous. Half the Brooklyn fans were still there celebrating. So they gave us the rush act all the way home on the subways and the elevated trains.

That was a beautiful windup to not such a good season. We finished sixth, although we played only five games under .500 ball. The next year we were fifth. That was as high as I got at Brooklyn. There was a dispute in the ownership at that time between the Ebbets and McKeever heirs, and they owed money to the Brooklyn Trust Company. So the club couldn't spend much money to buy ballplayers or build a farm system.

Bob Quinn, who was the business manager when I became manager, reminded me in a letter many years afterward: "Our instructions were not to purchase any players without permission from the Board of Directors, not even to claiming players on waiver, and the waiver price at that time in the National League was $6000."

We sometimes would hold tryouts for kids at the Brooklyn ball park in the mornings to see if we could find some local talent. We never did come up with much. There were some very peculiar cases. I'll never forget one man that went out to third base wearing shin guards.

I said, "Why don't you come back and catch batting practice! You're a catcher, aren't you?"

He said, "No, I'm a third baseman."

And I said, "Well, why have you got the shin guards on?"

And he said, "I've always been weak on ground balls."

Some of the best players I managed at Brooklyn were in their waning days. I had Johnny Frederick his last year, and also Hack Wilson. Wilson was a big-legged fellow who helped chase me off the New York Giants ten years before, then later did a very good job of hitting the ball with the Chicago Cubs under Joe McCarthy. He was the slugger type. He perspired very freely out there, had a good red face—it looked like the moon was coming up, see?

There's a story that's often been told about Hack Wilson in a game that was pitched for us by Walter Beck—or Boom Boom Beck, which is a nickname he got from a newspaper account of how he was shelled in this particular game.

It was in 1934 on June fifteenth. I remember the date because it was the trading deadline, and the newspapermen asked me before the game whether we were going to make any deals to strengthen the club. I said, "Well, to my knowledge, we're going to try to. We've got two or three deals on the fire."

They said, "Is the fire lit?" And they seemed very disturbed that we hadn't done anything or made any deals for the season.

Then they asked who was going to pitch that day, and when I said it was Walter Beck, they said, "Don't you know what his earned-run average is? It's too high." And he had been scored on a lot in a previous one-sided game.

This was in the old Baker Bowl in Philadelphia, where they had a short right field with a tin fence about a mile high that had a soap sign—CLEAN UP WITH LIFEBOY, or something like that. Hack Wilson was playing out there.

We got a four-run lead in the first inning, and then Walter Beck went out to pitch for us, and they came right back and got a couple of runs. And the next inning they had three men on base when the inning finally concluded.

I was getting burned up, after those writers had said I shouldn't pitch him. So I told Walter Beck, "I don't think you've got your stuff today. Maybe I should take you out. This is such a small bandbox park it's like hitting in a room. Why, they could make five or six runs any minute."

He was a very confident player, and he said, "Now listen. Don't go thinking of taking me out. I just commenced feeling good on those last hitters."

It went on like that. He'd get in trouble every inning, but a line-drive double play or something like that would save him, and he'd insist that his arm was loosening up and he was going to be all right.

Finally about the fifth inning, when it was boom, boom, and they had a couple of men on base again, I'd had enough. I walked out and said, "Walter, give me that ball."

He said, "No, sir, you let me pitch to this next hitter."

I said, "Walter, let me have that ball."

And he turned around and threw the ball out to right field, where Hack Wilson was playing. The ball hit that tin fence, and bing, it dropped off on the ground.

Hack evidently had been standing out there thinking about what he was going to do that night, because when he heard the ball hit that fence he turned around and chased it and fired it into second base. He thought the ball must have been pitched and hit. And everybody started to laugh and ridicule him, and that made him good and mad.

That's where people usually wind up the story, but there was more when Walter Beck finally came to the bench. I said, "Well, Walter, you were right about one thing. There's nothing wrong with your arm, or you wouldn't have been able to throw all the way out there to that fence."

He didn't say anything. He just went over and kicked over a pail of water. It splashed half the players on the bench, and they commenced scattering.

I said, "Walter, don't you dare kick that bucket again."

And Walter said, "Why won't I kick it?"

I said, "Because you might break your leg, and then I won't be able to sell or trade you."

I did trade him off a little later on to the Pacific Coast League. But he eventually came back to the big leagues, and after he finished pitching he was a great example as a coach.

He used to give this instruction to kids: "Don't get mad at your club. Don't get mad at your manager. When you sign a contract, do your best work. You don't want to go back to the minor leagues. The meals aren't as good, you don't get as good uniforms, you don't have as nice a clubhouse, you don't stay in as good hotels and you don't make as much money. So be sure you fight for your position all through the season. But if you do go down to the minors, you will always eventually have a chance to make a comeback. That's what I did when I went down the first time."

Another colorful player we had at Brooklyn was Frenchy Bordagaray. When he first reported to us in spring training in 1935 he had a dandy little mustache— it looked like a little French waiter had joined the club. And he had a red-haired girl for a wife, and she looked like a Hollywoodite.

He shaved the mustache off about the first month of the

season. I told him, "They're making fun of you now, and me too, with this mustache." So he shaved it off.

Bordagaray was a running fool. He could run, run, run. But he could shock you as a fielder in the outfield. One time a ball went out to him for the last out of a game. He put both hands up and the ball hit the top of his hands and bounced up in the air about fifteen feet. But he finally caught it—he reached up like a streetcar conductor going to pull the rope to ring up a fare, and he pulled the baseball down to him with one hand.

And he would sometimes shock you on the bases. In one game when I was coaching at third, Bordagaray was on second base, and he wanted to steal third. I kept giving him a sign—no, no. But he eventually went to steal anyway, and they threw him out.

Later in the game he was on second base again, and I said, "You stay there this time." And our hitter got a base hit and Bordagaray tried to score standing up, but he was thrown out at home plate.

I said to him, "Well, sir, there it is. You never should have been thrown out. They tell me you ran against a horse at one time"—which he did in the minors, for fifty yards. "If you could beat that horse, you ought to have beat that ball in to the plate."

He said, "Well, you wouldn't let me get off second base, so don't you go fining me for that."

I said, "All right, I'll fine you twenty-five dollars for not sliding."

He said, "Well, then you ought to fine yourself fifty dollars for sending me in."

After that, every time he'd get on base he'd run and make a big slide, whether he was fifty feet safe or not, and then look at me over at third as if to ask whether he was doing his work properly.

I used to try everything I could think of to win ball games with that Brooklyn team. Once we were leading the Giants but they were catching up to us. The weather was turning bad, and we tried to stall so that it would rain before they could beat us out. It got so dark I told the umpires, "You'd better call this game."

But they wouldn't do it. They were telling me to hurry up and get the game going. So I reached into the trainer's bag and took out the little flashlight that he had to look down a player's mouth if he had a sore throat. Then I signaled for a new pitcher to come in from the bullpen, and I used the flashlight to do it. I waved that up and down to show how dark it was.

The umpires didn't like that. They threw me out, and the next batter hit safe and the Giants beat us. So that was another time I got trimmed.

As I mentioned, my best pitcher at Brooklyn was Mungo. He could throw a ball and look like he was throwing lightning. Many times he'd strike out ten or twelve or fourteen men. So he was what I called my meal ticket. Traveling around with a second-division club, I'd pitch him in Chicago against one of their best pitchers. Then in St. Louis I'd have to pitch him against one of the Deans. Then when I got to New York City, I'd have to pitch him against Carl Hubbell.

Mungo won quite a few games, but with a not-so-good team behind him, he also would lose quite a few. At the start of 1936 there was an incident that disturbed him very much. We were playing an opening game in the Polo Grounds, and he's got the Giants beat, 2-1, in the last of the ninth. Then one of their men hits a high fly to the outfield, and our shortstop and left fielder run into each other. So the ball drops and Mungo loses the game. That made him want to tear up the clubhouse.

There were one or two other games where he didn't get very good support, and when we were getting up to the June fifteenth trading deadline he said, "I want to be traded." I said, "Listen, I just manage the team. I don't own the team. I can't trade you. I couldn't sign a paper, because no trade is any good unless it's got the owner's name on it."

Well, he got disturbed that night and jumped the team and went back to Brooklyn. He stayed there two or three days and they didn't trade him, so he decided later he'd join the team in Cincinnati.

I thought, "Well, he can't be in too good a shape after laying off like that. I'll just put him to work." And you can believe I really gave him plenty of work out there in practice to get him back in condition.

The business manager at Brooklyn, Bob Quinn, had left that year to become president of the Boston Braves. We finished down in seventh place, and after the season Jim Mulvey and Joe Gilleaudeau, two of the vice-presidents that were running the office, gave me the notification that my services weren't desired for the next year. They had one very good reason, which was that the club had not advanced in the pennant race.

I had known Mr. Mulvey since I first came to Brooklyn as a ballplayer more than twenty years before. I knew him and his wife, who was Dearie McKeever then. She was the daughter of one of the owners. We used to go over at night to her home, which had a brownstone front. Her mother would play the piano and Jim Mulvey would play the violin, and that was where I really learned to dance. And then we would have coffee and cake.

Mr. Mulvey says now about that 1936 firing, "Owing to the divided ownership and the interest of the bank in the financial affairs of the company, dissatisfaction arose with respect to the financial operations of the club, and one of the consequences was that Stengel was let go. In spite of that, Stengel and our family have been extremely close friends at all times."

I made a number of other good friends in Brooklyn. Some nice testimonial dinners were given for me while I was the manager, but one of the nicest was a dinner the New York and Brooklyn baseball writers put on four days after I got fired.

One of the speakers was Steve Owen, the coach of the pro football team in New York. He said, "Well, this is the greatest thing I ever saw. I've seen a man that has had a good year receive an award. I've seen a man that was a good fellow receive an award. But this is the first time I ever saw a man get an award for being discharged."

16

✂ Like Max Carey before me, I had another year on my contract when the Brooklyn club fired me after the 1936 season. Mr. Mulvey later made an agreement in which they would pay me my full $15,000 salary during 1937. So I became what you might call a W.P.A. manager. The joke in those depression times about the W.P.A., which was a government agency to make jobs for unemployed people, was that you got paid for not working.

I had a number of opportunities to go back to baseball in 1937. I was offered several managing jobs in the top minor leagues, and also a major-league coaching job, but I did not accept any of them. I went into the oil business down in Texas and stayed there most of the year.

I got into that through one of my ballplayers, Randy Moore. He'd been a terrific hitter against the Brooklyn club with Boston, and we'd made a trade to get him on our team for 1936. He played about forty games for me and then he broke his leg. So after he broke his leg he went down to the Texas oil fields with his father-in-law, Mr. Ferrier.

Randy Moore got me to come down there with him in

1937, and I used the money I was being paid for not managing Brooklyn. We'd go into different wells and take a small fraction of them. And it was a very good business. It turned out to be profitable for twenty years and more —in fact, some of the wells are still going.

And Randy Moore is still very successful. While it may be a terrible thing to say, he's probably better off that he broke his leg and got to leave baseball. He and his wife have been wonderful friends to me and some of his other baseball pals he brought into the oil business, like Al Lopez and John Cooney and Fred Frankhouse.

I was possibly going to give up baseball and stay in the oil business, but in 1938 I was invited back to the major leagues by Mr. Bob Quinn, who had left Brooklyn after 1935 to operate the Boston Braves. He invited me to become the manager. Their previous manager, Bill Mc-Kechnie, had accepted a job as manager of the Cincinnati ball team.

Mr. Quinn, whose son John now is general manager of the Phillies, died several years ago. He was one of my finest friends in baseball. He once wrote, "Stengel is the best teacher of baseball that I have ever worked with and the cleverest handler of men one could ask for. All he had to do was to be furnished with a half-decent respectable club and he could get more out of it than any manager I ever had."

We finished fifth my first year in Boston, but we won more than half our games. We had a team suited to our park. We couldn't hit the ball very hard, but neither could anybody else at Braves Field. The wind would blow in from left field off the Charles River and stop the balls from going very far. And we also would wet down the infield and put peat moss in it. We put so much peat moss in there that it took all the life out of a ground ball. In infield practice you'd have to swing hard just to hit fungoes to the infielders.

So we used to offset our lack of hitting with good out-fielders like Vince DiMaggio, who struck out a lot but could really catch and throw the ball; good infielders like Tony Cuccinello, and a good pitching staff and catching staff.

We had some pitchers that could keep the ball low— Jim Turner, Lou Fette, Danny MacFayden, Milt Shoffner. And I had Al Lopez as my number one catcher, who had caught for me before in Brooklyn, and Lopez was one of the best catchers in baseball. He was a terrific man for the pitchers, because he could catch those low pitches and make them look good to the umpires.

So at home we'd seldom get beat worse than 1-0, 3-2, 4-3—we never had many high-scoring games. But when we went on the road it was very sad. With those hard in-fields, the balls would get through, and my team couldn't hit the home runs. And we got a pretty good scalping on the road.

After the 1938 season I was down in Texas in December when I got word that my mother had died in Kansas City. I got up there as fast as I could by plane for the funeral. She was seventy-seven, and she and my father had been married for almost fifty-three years. My dad survived her by about a year and a half—he also passed away while I was the Boston manager.

I had that job for six years. We had trouble rivaling the Boston Red Sox in attendance. They had great slug-gers then, and a short fence in left field, and no wind to bother them. And I was told that we should try to get more hitters.

In 1938, the year the Red Sox first took Ted Williams to training camp, we got Max West. The year before that, when I was out of baseball, I had seen Williams play at San Diego. Bill McKechnie, who was managing the Braves then, asked me to go look at him. Williams at that time was eighteen or nineteen. I watched him hit, and I told McKechnie, "You don't need me as a coach"—he'd offered me a job after I left Brooklyn—"what you need is a man of the ability of this Williams." But the Red Sox had already made a deal with the San Diego club to get him.

So I tried to rival Williams with Max West, and he played very good ball for me. Our park was too large for his fielding ability, but he could hit a ball out of sight, and was my leading home-run hitter. I remember that in the 1940 All Star Game in St. Louis, in which he got a home run that won the game for the National League, he ran into the fence and hurt his spine. That hampered his later career, and I understand that today he wears a brace.

I also had Paul Waner in Boston when he got his three-thousandth hit in 1942. He was getting old, but he was still an amazing hitter. If a pitcher threw at him, he'd say, "I'll knock him down myself." And he'd hit a line drive back at the pitcher and come pretty close to scalping him.

The club didn't improve during my six years in Boston. If anything, it went down. Mr. Quinn and I were financially handicapped, much the same as we had been in Brooklyn. This club had an owner with money, Mr. C. F. Adams. But he also owned the Suffolk Downs race track, and in those days, if you were in the racing business where there was gambling, Commissioner Landis didn't want you in the baseball business. So Mr. Adams couldn't give us the money to sign young players, because the minute he started doing it, Landis was going to make all the players free agents, which he had done to clubs on other occasions.

We had to do as much selling as buying. Frank Frisch was managing at Pittsburgh then. I sold him a couple of players, and they didn't do too good. Frisch said, "If I ever let you sell me any more men like that, you can just walk up and hit me in the eye."

But I finally did sell him another player in 1941 for about ten or twelve thousand dollars. It was a pitcher named Joe Sullivan. Frisch got very disturbed about this man too. It seems he was looking for him on the field before a game in Brooklyn once, and he wasn't anywhere in sight. They finally found him curled up asleep inside the big roller that was used for the tarpaulin.

Judge Landis had made a statement that Mr. Adams, the Boston owner, should either get out of baseball or get out of racing, and Adams finally decided to sell the ball club. He gave a group of us a chance to buy him out—the Perini brothers, Joe Maney, Guido Rugo, Bob Quinn and his son John, and also myself. I first put in $25,000, and then I put in $25,000 more. I'd say that for about $250,000 cash we started taking possession of the ball club, but eventually, it commenced being purchased by Mr. Lou Perini from the rest of us.

When the Perini boys took over at the end of 1943, Mr. Quinn told me, "It looks like they want to change managers. But I'm staying, and if you want to, I'll see that you stay here this next year."

I said to him, "No, I wouldn't want to handicap anybody." So I went to New York City and had a meeting with Lou Perini. I had $11,000 coming in salary, and $25,000 of my own money that was still in the club, and I got it all paid off.

That last year in Boston I had physical troubles too. Just before the season opened we played the Red Sox in an exhibition game and won it, and were rather proud that we did. That night I wanted to talk to two or three men that had just joined the club. There was a heavy rain and there was a dimout on at night, because this was during wartime. And when I went to go across the street to this hotel, holding a newspaper over my head, I stopped at a sort of V in the middle of the street to let an automobile go by. This driver didn't see me, evidently, because he started to go one way and then he decided to go the other way, and he turned quick and caught me on the leg.

That put me in the hospital for several months. One of the Boston writers, who didn't care for my work as manager, put in his paper that this was the greatest thing that had happened to the ball club since I came there.

I had my coaches, George Kelly and Bob Coleman, run the team while I was in the hospital, and they did as well as I could have done myself. After I was laid up for about three months I foolishly got up and decided to make a road trip with my leg in a cast. I wanted to get out of bed after having my leg propped up so long (during which a large knot accumulated on it). They put on a new cast before I left, and it was too tight—after six weeks I found out it was killing the life of my leg. Then I had to have the cast cut off, and the leg was so weak I had to wear a brace for some months afterward.

It looked for a time like I might lose my leg. On three or four occasions doctors suggested that I lose it. But I came home to Glendale after the season and worked on that leg all winter. I'd put it in the swimming pool and try to freeze it somewhat, and then I'd come in and put it in a pail of hot water. And I walked backward up hills, which made me stretch out my toes.

The leg began to come around, but I decided I would not take a baseball job in 1944. I had several opportunities but turned them down.

Up in Milwaukee, which was in the American Association in those days, Charlie Grimm was running the ball club in partnership with Bill Veeck. Mr. Veeck had gone into the military service, and then after the 1944 season opened, Grimm was invited to come back to Chicago as manager of the Cubs.

Grimm called me up and said, "I have three days to accept this position with the Cubs. I wouldn't mind taking it if you will take over at Milwaukee for me." He said that with him and his partner both away they'd need an experienced man there.

I said I didn't think I wanted to, but he kept calling me, and finally I said yes. So I went to Milwaukee in May of '44, and to tell you the truth, it was a good-looking team. Everywhere I'd managed before I'd taken teams that were down in the standings, but this club was in first place.

I was still limping very badly, but I never wore a brace on the coaching lines. And I guess it was a good thing I took the brace off at that time, because my leg got strong again. I've never needed a brace for it since, although I still have that big knot at the bottom of my shin —it looks like an apple.

One night there in Milwaukee a man went out and imitated me coaching on third—with gestures, and rolling his arms and eyes. And he took a baseball and put it down his stocking, and everybody seemed to get great fun out of that. I said, "Do I look that bad?" But I guess I did.

Bill Veeck and Charlie Grimm had been running that club in wonderful shape, and built up tremendous interest by the public. When Veeck first heard out in the South Pacific that Grimm had left me in charge, he was very disturbed. He wrote a letter, of which I've seen a copy, in which he said he didn't have any use for my services.

Mr. Veeck and I didn't know each other then, but we later became very friendly. When he came back and saw that we'd won the pennant in 1944, kept up the attendance and sold almost everybody off the club to the major leagues, he offered me the opportunity to manage again in 1945.

But I had already resigned. Right after the season I gave a dinner for the ballplayers. Then I gave one for the writers—they told me Veeck and Grimm used to do that. After it was all over, about four o'clock in the morning, I said, "Now you can all go to work instead of going home."

They said, "Why?"

I said, "I've resigned. I'm not going to manage here next year."

So they all had to write a story about that instead of going to bed, the poor writers.

I signed in 1945 with the Kansas City club, which was the New York Yankees' farm team in the same league. I went there for the main purpose of paying off some debts to George Weiss, the Yankee farm director. I told you how I'd known him since 1925 in the Eastern League.

And later on, when I was with clubs that didn't have cash to buy players I needed, he sold some of them to me on time payments. One was Buddy Hassett, a first baseman that played for me at Brooklyn, and another was Eddie Miller, a first-class shortstop I had at Boston.

Mr. Weiss had done more favors for me over the years than anybody—him and Mr. McGraw. The other clubs were very fair with me too, except that I had to put out, naturally, cash money.

The Yankees didn't have too much talent on their Kansas City farm that year. I took a last-place club and we had a good fighting team in 1945, and sold off three players to the big leagues. But we only finished seventh.

And after that season I resigned again. I had paid off my obligation to Weiss. And again I didn't know whether I would stay in baseball.

17

✂ They say the big leagues are the only place to be in baseball, but I also had some good positions in the minor leagues. One of them turned up after I re-signed from Kansas City at the end of 1945. I went back home to Glendale, and Cookie de Vincenzi, who had been the owner of the Oakland club in the Pacific Coast League, came to see me.

He said, "I remember when I had Ernie Lombardi, and you helped me sell him to the big leagues about fifteen years ago. Well, the position of manager at Oakland is open, and I'd like to introduce you to the new owners, Brick Laws and Joe Blumenfeld."

Pants Rowland, who had been a manager in the Northern Association when I broke into professional ball at Kankakee back in 1910, was president of the Coast League, and he said, "I'm going to recommend you to those two men myself."

So I talked with them a couple of times, and I decided that I would accept the position for 1946. Evidently they were satisfied with my services, because this is what Brick Laws wrote when he was asked to say something about me for this story:

I first met Casey at my home in late '45, and one of the first things I asked was, "How long do you think it will take you to win or become a contender in Oakland?" His reply in effect: "It will take me a year to learn the league, another year to develop and buy players to compete, and then with a little luck I can win it in the third." His prediction came true exactly as anticipated, for Oakland moved immediately into the first division and in the third year won the Pacific Coast League championship for the first time in twenty-one years.

In my twelve years in baseball I never saw a manager who had a more burning desire to win. I have sat up with Casey until three or four in the morning during a losing streak, and then seen him awake at seven with fresh and new ideas on who to play, how to change the batting line-up, and so forth.

It was a very interesting job, as the fight in the Coast League was red-hot in those days. The Los Angeles team was a very good team, and there also was a very good team in San Francisco, where Lefty O'Doul was the manager. He had been one of the best hitters for average in the big league. He was a good teacher, and had numerous friends all over the Pacific Coast—he was one of the most popular men in the state of California.

O'Doul was doing such a good job at San Francisco, and interest built up so much at Oakland, that one year they drew 660,000 for the season at home, and our ball club drew 630,000. And just think, three or four years later you couldn't draw 100,000 in either park.

Every Monday was an off day in the Pacific Coast League, and that was a very hard thing for me to get used to as a manager. In other words, if you started your number one and number two pitchers on Tuesday and Wednesday, you could pitch them again on Saturday and Sunday. But then the next week you didn't know who to open up with on Tuesday. So you had to be very careful how you handled a pitching staff to keep it in good working order. I found after the first year that I could run it a little better.

I had old men and young men on that team, and some people think that's where my platooning started, but actually I'd been doing it whenever I could since the 1920's in Toledo.

You remember how the United States Supreme Court used to be called "The Nine Old Men"? Well, some of the writers gave our Oakland team that nickname because we had so many older players on it when we won the pennant in 1948. They'd say before a game, "Well, Case, you got those old boys here today? Tell 'em to kick their legs around a little so we'll know they're still alive."

I bought Ernie Lombardi back to catch at Oakland, and I also had another catcher that assisted me greatly —Bill Raimondi. He was very bright and knew all the other players' weaknesses, because he'd been in the league ten or fifteen years. Then I had Cookie Lavagetto at Oakland, and Dario Lodigiani. I had Jim Tobin and Les Scarsella, Nick Etten and Maurice Van Robays.

One of the young players I took access to was Billy Martin. One day I put his name in the line-up hitting eighth, and he said, "Is that your line-up? Is that where I'm supposed to hit?"

And I said, "Yeah, that's my line-up. And that's where you're supposed to hit."

He said, "Well, what do you think I am, the ground-keeper? I shouldn't be hitting eighth. I hit .392 last year." Which he did do in 1947 out at Phoenix in the Arizona-Texas League. And he became a very good second baseman for me.

My first year there, 1946, Mr. Weiss of the Yankees let me have a pitcher, Frank Shea, who did a great job for us and then went up and helped them win the pennant in 1947. And I also had Gene Bearden, who helped pitch Cleveland to the pennant in 1948. He had not too much speed, but he had a knuckle ball. I convinced him to pitch low, and he always thanked me for that afterward.

Then I had a man named Ralph Buxton that was a pretty good pitcher. The other teams used to claim that he used a tar ball. They said he would put a little piece of tar on the baseball to give it an extra twist. One time when we were fighting San Francisco for the pennant, and playing in their park, about twenty-five guys came out of the grandstand and down on the field before the game to try and embarrass him. Each one had a sand bucket like little kids take to the beach, and the buckets were filled with tar.

Later I had Buxton for a while with the Yankees, and I'll have to say he helped us in a special way. He tipped off one or two of my pitchers—I don't want to give their names—on how a man could put a little piece of tar on the end of his fingernail, and it would stick on the baseball and make it do a little flip. Anyway, it was rumored that at times a pitcher would throw one, and it's possible that it did happen.

When I was managing at Oakland I still used to go out on the third-base coaching line, and when I was out there I would always try to coke it up. "Coking it up" means jumping up in the air and being alive and shouting at your players. Or you could yell at the other team's player to distract him, or maybe talk to him and get his mind off the game.

People used to say, "Well, Stengel's full of life, anyway."

I even heard that later with the Yankees when I was managing from the bench. We had four or five men there that were quiet—great players, but quiet. When we were in a losing streak, George Weiss used to say to me, "You're the only fellow I hear yelling in there. See if you can't make the coaches yell, and some of the ballplayers, even if they've never yelled in their lives."

Sometimes in the minor leagues when I was coaching at third and there was a bad decision, I'd fall over like I'd fainted dead away from the shock. I also tried that in the big leagues a couple of times, but the umpires didn't like it. They stopped me from doing it.

There was one pitcher I used to do a pretty good job of imitating out at Oakland. He was a schoolteacher, and every Sunday he'd come down and pitch for Sacramento. And he'd drive me crazy, because he held us spellbound. He went through so many motions before he delivered the ball to the plate that my hitters would start to swing too soon.

So I commenced yelling at him from the coaching lines and trying to ridicule him by going through the same motions. But we never did beat him until the last two games he pitched against us. And I think he beat us about eight times.

As I mentioned, the Oakland job had a number of advantages. It was fairly close to home, and Edna enjoyed the trips up and down the Coast. There had been a period of eleven years when we couldn't be together very much during the baseball season. Her mother got very sick, after having been in an automobile accident, and became bedridden. Edna acted as her mother's nurse and did a very good job of it. So during the season we only saw each other on short visits.

In the Oakland job, which came after Edna's mother had passed away, it was different. I thought this might be where I would end up my career in baseball. But it turned out that the biggest part of it was still to come.

We finished second, then fourth and then first in my three years at Oakland. The Yankees had two great scouts on the West Coast. One was Bill Essick in Los Angeles and the other was Joe Devine in San Francisco. They evidently sent favorable reports on my work to George Weiss, who had advanced from farm director to general manager of the Yankees.

And then my Oakland boss, Brick Laws, used to play golf with Del Webb. Mr. Webb was one of the owners of the Yankees. He was a contractor with some building contracts in that territory.

One day Del Webb told Brick Laws that the Yankees were interested in my services as manager. They had lost the pennant under Bucky Harris in 1948, and during the World Series they announced that they were letting Harris go.

A few days later I was told, "They want you to come to New York City." I went there with Brick Laws. We were put in the Waldorf-Astoria Hotel, and we stayed two nights. I had two or three conversations with the Yankee owners—Mr. Webb and Mr. Dan Topping. We agreed on salary, and we agreed on a two-year contract, and then they took me over to a luncheon for the writers and broadcasters at the "21" Club.

A lot of people say it was Mr. Webb's idea to get me as the Yankee manager. I think it was Mr. Weiss who had the most to do with it. He had known me since 1925. Of course, there's no question that I also knew Mr. Webb, and I also got to know Mr. Topping. And those two owners had to approve of it.

Well, in 1949 I was a strange new manager coming into the American League for the first time in my life. And I was about to change the New York Yankees over from any system that had been used there in the past. This is no knock on Bucky Harris's system before me, or on Joe McCarthy's system before him. Mr. McCarthy was a great manager—he won eight pennants with the Yankees in fifteen years. He was a good personal friend of mine—had been for years—and I admired his ability. A lot of the talent he developed was still on the Yankees when I got there.

But I had to find out how to use this talent to win my way. I had to play my own system. And my system was platooning.

I used to play with the dead ball, and this gives me a different slant than some of the other managers. I saw baseball change with a lively ball, and I watched men manage with a lively ball. I found out you had to have different methods in pitching, you had to have different methods of how to run a game. And you had to execute so as to get the best out of each player, even if it did embarrass him at times. That meant platooning him, which will cause embarrassment every day.

I know a lot of the players never understood my platoon system, and neither did a lot of other people. They say that now that I'm through running the Yankees, there won't be so much platooning in baseball. Well, I'll say this —I don't think we'd have won the ten pennants in my twelve years without it.

18

When I signed to manage the Yankees, Mr. Webb and Mr. Topping told me that Mr. Weiss would be the man that was in charge of things, and that I would work under him in making deals, and so on and so forth. Naturally, if a deal involved a large sum of money, I suppose he got in touch with the owners first and told them about it. And that's the way the situation went along for many years. It wasn't until much later that there was any friction with the owners.

I had a verbal agreement with them—I don't have it in writing and they don't—that if in one year they didn't like my work too well or I didn't like their methods, I could leave despite the two-year contract.

Except in my year at Milwaukee in the American Association, where we won the pennant in 1944, this was the first time I had ever taken over a team that was up in the standings. The Yankees had finished third behind Cleveland and Boston in 1948. But not too much was expected of them in 1949. In a vote of 206 baseball writers before the season, 119 picked the Boston club to win under Joe McCarthy, and 79 voted for Cleveland. There were only six that picked us. But I thought myself that we could win. We had some real talent if I could handle it right.

I started right in with my platooning. I had to platoon a man like Tommy Henrich, who could play first base or the outfield, because he had a knee that would get out of the socket. And I used to have to platoon Charlie Keller in the outfield because he had a bad spine. He could come out and play as hard as ever, but he'd get a stiff back and couldn't sleep at night.

That Keller—I want to tell you, that boy thought he could hit, and showed it the way he stood up at the plate, and he could hit. Henrich was also a sharp hitter. He generally got the pitch he wanted. No matter how many strikes the pitcher threw, Henrich would foul enough of them off so he finally got a fast ball he could do a very beautiful job with.

These were two great players, and I platooned them because of age and physical condition. With a man that is getting aged, if you rest him every so often you will find that he commences getting limber again with his muscles. His legs are fresh, and he can run fast again for five or six days. And he's quicker with the bat.

So I had to bring along other men to rest them. In the outfield I had an experienced man, John Lindell, who played left field. He could hit a ball a mile, and was aggressive and a good-spirited man on a ball club. Then I had Cliff Mapes. He was a good thrower in right field, and could hit the ball fairly good.

Then we also were getting new outfielders like Hank Bauer and Gene Woodling. Bauer was right-handed, and he was not a curve-ball hitter when he started, but he improved on it. Woodling was left-handed, and he eventually became a terrific hitter because he wasn't afraid at the plate.

Now another thing about platooning is this. Many times young ballplayers have been humiliated by being brought along too fast. Then you have a man that will blow up on you over the season. So one of the biggest jobs when you're the manager is how to handle the young ballplayer who has not quite made it, but thinks he has.

In his own mind he can hit any pitcher. So he gives you a great fight at the plate. He doesn't realize that he can't hit an expert pitcher yet—that he is not only being fooled, but those balls are coming in with too much stuff for him to handle, too much curve and so forth.

If he stays in there long enough to find that out, then he loses confidence in himself, and that's a terrible thing. I always wanted to prevent that if I could, and I would platoon the young man on his mental condition.

So I said when I first started with the Yankees, "These older men are wearing down now—the one with the knee, Henrich, and the other with the back, Keller. So I'll blend these young men in. I can platoon them, and they'll be more confident."

They will also be mad at the manager, because the manager didn't play them regular. I didn't like to see it, but it did happen with a number of men. They just had to realize that the best way to show the manager up is by working hard and keeping in shape, so you can play well when you do get the chance.

I know McGraw expected you to stay in condition if you were a utility player. He didn't want you to go in there and have a bad day and then say, "Don't blame me for not doing good. Blame the manager. He hasn't played me in twenty days."

McGraw's idea was that if you keep working out hard every day, then you'll always be in shape to play. Your wind is good. You can catch a ball. You can throw a ball. You don't have a sore arm. You may be off in hitting, because you don't get regular big-league hitting practice every day, but you can come out and take extra practice in the morning.

I think Woodling was brought up where he had the nerve and the fight, and so was Bauer. After I platooned those men, they eventually got to where they had to play regular, because they could hit the good pitchers in the American League. Previous to that they only hit fairly good against them.

In center field, just think, I had Joe DiMaggio. I'd never had a player that great before. Well, naturally you don't platoon a man like DiMaggio. But he had what was known as a bone spur on his heel at that time. In spring training he went to a hospital in Baltimore to get it treated. Then when he came back and went out on the ball field, wearing a special shoe, he found he couldn't put his foot down without it hurting him. So he missed the first sixty-five games of the 1949 season, and we had to do plenty of platooning out there until he got well enough to play.

When it came to the infield, numerous men told me that Joe McCarthy, who had handled the Yankees for so many years, was one of the finest managers there'd ever been at handling an infield, and perhaps he was. But I had to make new infielders almost every year, and I had my own methods.

Some managers have one special way they want double plays to be made. My system was, make it any way you can. But be sure you find some way to make it, or I can't play you. I told the infielders that, and had my coaches telling them, and it ended up that we generally had good double-play men on the Yankees, except maybe in 1959.

At shortstop when I started we had Rizzuto. That was another man I never platooned. Rizzuto had somewhat hurt his arm previously, which had handicapped the club during the 1948 pennant race. He could go to his right very speedily, but I was told by some of the players at spring training that it had become pretty hard for him to throw a man out after he went way deep for a ball over toward third base.

I watched him in training camp and suggested that he loft the ball to get it over there. And he did whether I wanted him to or not. The big thing is not what the manager tells you, but what you do about it yourself. And he perfected a system in which he could get rid of the ball with an amazing quick throw. It would fly in the air, but he'd get rid of it so fast it would beat the runner. And that sometimes is better than an infielder who catches the ball, takes too long to throw it, and then throws a bullet over to first base.

Rizzuto could do everything else except, maybe, hit for distance. So he was a very good shortstop for me for several years.

At second base I had George Stirnweiss, a good, fast man on the bases, and also a very good man fielding. But he didn't give us too much punch at the plate, and then he hurt his hand and wrist during the season. So I had to use Gerry Coleman at second base.

People told me, "Coleman can't hit enough." But he would fight at the plate. He got so that he was vicious up there. Coleman wore his uniform a lot like Frank Crosetti, the Yankee shortstop under McCarthy, who had become a coach. Instead of putting their baseball trousers way down near their ankles like some of the other ballplayers, they would roll their pants right over their knees. That way the umpires were less likely to call low strikes on them, which made them harder to pitch to.

And Coleman was a good double-play man. He threw beautiful overhanded. He could jump up in the air, and while he was in the air he could throw to first base over-handed, and he was very accurate. He was just like a great basketball player that can jump up in the air and make a perfect shot.

Then I had two splendid third basemen—Billy Johnson and Bobby Brown. Johnson hit right-handed and Brown hit left-handed. Johnson had an amazing arm to first base—never threw bad—and could hit an extra base hit occasionally. And when I put Brown in, he could tattoo some of the good pitchers. Brown was a medical student during the winter and never could report on time in spring training, and that handicapped him somewhat to become a regular. But I could platoon him with Johnson, and that worked very good in 1949.

At first base I made a mistake. Bill Skiff, a very capable man in the Yankee organization, saw the making of a first baseman in Joe Collins, but I didn't listen enough to Skiff in training, and I farmed Collins out most of that year. I used Dick Kryhoski and Jack Phillips quite a bit at first base, but finally I settled down mostly to Henrich. I had been playing Henrich in right field, but he was just as good at first base, and it was easier for me to find another right fielder than another good first baseman.

This 1949 club didn't have as much hitting punch in the infield and the outfield as some of the great Yankee teams of the past, so I decided that Berra had to be the catcher. Berra had not done so well throwing and had been awkward behind the plate against Brooklyn in the 1947 World Series, and in 1948 they tried making him an outfielder. But I found that he could go back and become a first-string catcher. Later on I platooned Berra at other positions, but his first seven years for me he caught practically all our games.

The job of making a good catcher out of Berra was given in spring training to Bill Dickey. Dickey had been a great Yankee catcher himself, naturally, and we signed him up as a coach.

I didn't pick my own coaches when I took over the Yankees. Sometimes later I wished that I had. But at the time I didn't know many coaches who were familiar with the American League. And I didn't want to bring in strange coaches, since I was a stranger to the league myself. So I decided to go by the recommendations of Mr. Weiss, with the understanding that if I wasn't satisfied with the work of the men he brought in, they would not stay one full season.

There had been four coaches on the Yankees in 1948. One of them, Charlie Dressen, left to take my previous job as manager at Oakland. Red Corriden also left, and so did John Schulte, who had been the bullpen coach. The only one that stayed on was Frank Crosetti. He became our third-base coach, and he also could coach infielders.

So we had to hire some more coaches. Mr. Weiss said, "Maybe Dickey will come here. I'd like to have Dickey back on the ball club." That sounded like a very good idea to me. And Mr. Dickey steadied Berra and helped him become the best catcher in the league, and he also was successful for a number of years in training other catchers. Where other clubs couldn't find catchers, we always had extra ones to trade, like Clint Courtney and Gus Triandos and Hal Smith. And later we came up with Elston Howard and Johnny Blanchard.

At the beginning there, in addition to Berra, our catchers were Charlie Silvera and Ralph Houk. While they were good men, they could not hit the ball for distance the way Berra did, so most of the time they had to become what you'd call assistant coaches out in the bullpen.

With the outfielders I did most of the coaching myself. I had my own ideas about outfielding. There were three experienced men that didn't need any teaching or any managerial guidance—DiMaggio, Henrich and Keller —but the newer men did.

That left the pitching staff. As our pitching coach we hired Jim Turner. He had pitched for me back when I was running the Boston club in the National League. Later he had experience managing in the minors. When I was at Oakland he was a very good manager over at Portland. During the 1947 season there he had helped develop Vic Raschi, who was now one of the star pitchers of the Yankees, so that was another good reason for having Turner on the club.

Raschi was the greatest pitcher I ever had to be sure to win. It looked like we would never make any mistakes when he was pitching. And he never would give in any time that he pitched, even when his stuff was ordinary. That's why he was a nine-inning pitcher.

He wasn't a graceful pitcher—he just put so much on it. If there were one, two or three men on bases, Raschi stuck and stuck and fought it out, and before three-and-two something would happen. A swinging roller would be hit, or maybe they'd hit a line drive at somebody. But this man just would not give in.

Then there was Allie Reynolds. He became an amazing pitcher for me. He could start games, and he also got so that he could come in and finish them in relief. When I first came to New York they said Reynolds couldn't go the distance very often. But he got so that he did. He was a terrific competitor, and wasn't afraid of any batter that ever walked up to the plate. The men that hit Reynolds best were the little cheap hitters like Nelson Fox, not the slugger hitters. I never was afraid with Reynolds when the big, strong hitters were up there.

So there were two great pitchers. Then we had another first-class starting pitcher in Lopat. And I suppose you remember Joe Page. There was a man they called the fireman, because he came in and put the fires out in the late innings. He did an amazing job in relief.

I believe in platooning with relief pitchers. Early in this story, when I was talking about the differences between baseball with the dead ball and baseball with the lively ball, I told you why pitchers can't start and finish games as often as they used to. So why strain a starting pitcher by keeping him in there when you're going to need him over a long pennant race?

I'd rather not wait too long to take a pitcher out. I will often take him out if the other team hit the ball hard the inning before, even if the balls were caught—unless it's a case where he has an eight- or ten-run lead and he's just tossing the ball up there and letting them hit it, to save his arm for the late innings.

But if I see in the sixth inning, say, that he's pumping and throwing his hardest and yet they're still hitting him,

I'll put another man in the next inning, because I figure he'll go worse from then on. And when the second pitcher goes in there, I'll have a third one warming up. So if my second pitcher walks the first two hitters or something like that, then I have a third shot at stopping the other team.

Of course, some people said I changed pitchers too much. There's the argument about the platoon system again.

Anyway, there was another big reason why I platooned with relief pitchers. I like good pinch hitters. I believe that with a lively ball you've got to be an attacker. If I've got a good pinch hitter, I hate to have him stay on the bench with men on the bases in an early inning. He may end the game right there. He may make them take out their pitcher—a good pitcher that would otherwise have gone nine innings—because he popped him at the right time.

I prefer to get ahead of somebody early and then have them try to catch me. I don't want them getting a three- or four-run lead on me at the beginning, because then they know how to play against me. They know I'm not going to bunt for a run, or anything like that.

But if they do get ahead of you four-to-nothing, what's the use of staying with your best pitchers and your best defensive men? You have to start platooning with men that can hit. Of course, sometimes you'll catch up to them, and then in the ninth inning one of the hitters you've put in will boot a ball on defense, and you lose anyway. But you'd never have even been in the game without him.

It isn't only the pitchers that need relief under modern conditions, with so many of the games lasting three to four hours, instead of two hours or less as in the old days.

So when you get into those long doubleheaders on hot summer days, it often is a good idea to platoon some of your ballplayers in the second game, to help them stay fresh and alert over the season.

There was criticism of all these things while I was managing the Yankees. But what caused more arguments than anything else was the way I kept shifting my line-ups and batting orders from game to game. I couldn't explain too much about it at the time. There were more things that entered into it than most people knew.

19

✂ Well, why *didn't* I stick to a set line-up when I was managing the Yankees? Why did I change things around from day to day? The answer is that the situation changes from day to day. If all your players were in the DiMaggio and Mantle class it wouldn't matter, but you never have a whole team of men like that. So to get the most out of your material, every day you build a line-up according to the situation for that particular game.

First you start off with who's pitching for the other team. It isn't just a matter of using your left-handed hitters against a right-handed pitcher, and so forth. You probably will do that if it's a side-arm right-handed pitcher, because he generally does bother the right-hand hitters more—it looks like he's throwing at the batter's head when he's cross-firing from third base. But if it's a right-handed pitcher with an overhand curve ball, some right-hand hitters can handle him better than some of the left-handers.

Then again, while you usually prefer right-handed hitters against a left-handed pitcher, not many of them can hit a left-hander with a good screw ball, like Carl Hubbell used to have.

If a top pitcher is in there, I'm very careful that I don't put a weak hitter up in the batting order. If I want the man in the game for his fielding ability, but I see that he's somewhat timid against a good pitcher—a vicious pitcher —I put him down the list.

It gets some people's goat when I move men up and down the batting order. But it doesn't get mine, because if a man is a weak hitter, or a green hitter, I have him batting eighth, where he'll only come up three times instead of four. Or I can pinch-hit for him late in the game. It's a dangerous thing to have a green hitter batting eighth in an important situation. They'll often pitch to him rather than to your pitcher, because they can make him chase bad pitches.

You also platoon your hitters according to the ball park. In Yankee Stadium I always liked left-handed hitters because of the short right field. If the other team started a pitcher I didn't think was too good against left-handed hitters, I liked to have them batting second, third, fourth and fifth.

But if the pitcher was so fast they couldn't pull the ball to right field, then I'd rather have right-handed hitters that could hit to the opposite field. And if you send up too many left-handed hitters in Yankee Stadium, then everybody's going to go out and find nothing but left-handed pitchers to start and finish games against you. So you want to have some right-hand hitters in your line-up, and you always want to save some for pinch-hitting in the late innings—especially men that can hit the ball to right.

For your lead-off hitter, you like to have a man that can get bases on balls. Now people don't realize this, but I never had a good base-on-balls man to lead off on the Yankees except for Rizzuto the first few years. You look up the records of the Yankees for the last ten years, and you'll see they all want to hit on one-and-nothing, two-and-nothing, three-and-nothing.

Rizzuto also could bunt, so people said I should have him bat second for sacrifices. But to tell you the truth, Rizzuto could bunt a ball better on his own for a hit than he could to sacrifice. I didn't know that at first, but I found it out.

Your number two hitter should be a man that can hit behind the runner—hit the ball to right field with a man on first. If he's left-handed, he has to be able to pull the ball. If he's a right-handed hitter, he has to be able to hit to right.

In the middle of your batting order you want men that can slug the ball. But you should never have two slow-footed, right-handed sluggers batting one after the other, because the double plays will murder you. If one of them gets on first, the other team will play the next man to hit the ball to the left side of the infield. And when he does, the runner from first base can't get down to second base fast enough to interfere with the pivot man in completing the double play.

In 1960 I got Roger Maris to pair up with Mickey Mantle in my batting order. Maris is a left-handed slugger who had a tremendous first half of the season, but he was out for a while with a rib injury in the second half, and then he got a little off against left-handed pitching. So I had him bat third and had Mantle hit after him, because if they put a left-hander in to pitch to Maris, he had also to pitch to Mantle, who is a home-run hitter right-handed or left-handed.

Actually, I'd have preferred it the other way around. Mantle is so fast that if he gets on base the next man can score him on a single or double, where others need a double or triple. He also can go first to third, where a fly ball will score him, or he'll go into second on a force-out and break up the double play.

And it makes it better for Maris too. He hits the ball to right field. Now if Mantle is on first, the first baseman has to play on the bag, or Mantle would steal second just like that. So Maris is hitting without a first baseman. Berra is another left-handed hitter who is helped by that. It's easier for him when a runner is being held on first base.

Some men hit best against a pitcher that keeps the ball low—a sinker-ball pitcher. Other hitters like the ball up high. Whatever kind of pitcher the other team starts, you try to send the kind of hitters against him that are going to give him the most trouble.

Only you don't choose a line-up just for hitting their pitcher. You do some platooning for defense, too. If your own pitcher is a left-hander who throws a lot of curves and keeps the ball low, then you want to have good fielders on the infield at second, short and third. Not only will your pitcher have them hitting the ball on the ground, but being a left-hander, it's easier for him to hold runners on first. So you should have extra chances to make double plays.

Or suppose the other club puts a second-rate catcher in there for his hitting. Then I'll build my batting order for speed. I'll have my fast men up at the top of the list. If they can get on base they'll bother that catcher. And that will bother the pitcher too.

So there are many different ways of platooning your line-up. And the more familiar I became with the American League the more of it I did.

Getting back to my first year with the Yankees in '49,

it looked at the beginning like I should take it easy and not do too much managing, because we had so many experienced players that didn't need any instruction. I think one of the first times I really started managing that ball team was when the Brooklyn club showed us up in some spring exhibition games.

Brooklyn had some first-class talent. Pee Wee Reese was a great base runner. As a base stealer, he'd only get caught five times in twenty to thirty attempts. Jackie Robinson was a sensational base runner. He was a thrill-runner. He'd get on base and he'd bluff you, then he'd give it a run and be safe.

Now Hodges, of course, didn't have to steal bases, and Snider didn't. And I don't say Campanella was a great base runner, but he was a slick catcher. He looked like he had a fat stomach, but that stomach didn't bother him at all. He was a nimble man. And he was a splendid low-ball catcher—he could squat behind home plate with his fanny actually touching the ground.

Another thing about Campanella was the fact that he had a very good disposition. He came up when we first commenced having Negroes in the big league, and I think he got by with as little trouble, for being a catcher, as anybody possibly could. When you're catching you can get in trouble no matter what your color is, because you've got to block a runner off from home plate, and he's got to knock you down when he runs in.

Anyway, where the Brooklyn club really shocked us in 1949 spring training was in running the bases. There was nobody in the American League—the White Sox hadn't started it yet—that could say, "Go, Go, Go!" Our pitchers hadn't been brought up in the American League to have perfection in holding men on the bases, and the new pitchers we had from the minor leagues had poor moves to first base, second base, third base. So our pitchers were embarrassed in those exhibition games, and the infielders, and it also made Berra look bad as a catcher again, because the pitchers did nothing to protect him.

The worst part of it was that the pitchers began watching the base runners so closely that they put nothing on the ball when they threw it to the plate. They were trying to catch those men jumping up on the base paths, like Robinson and Reese, and the men that were killing us were the men with the bats.

So I called our team together, and I said, "There's one thing I can tell you you're weak on. There haven't been any base-running teams to test you." And that gave us something to practice on all year, and things were pretty well straightened around by the time of the World Series, in which we beat that Brooklyn club four games to one.

In the World Series, Brooklyn wasn't getting the home runs, except in one game out of the five. And there were less men on the bases to steal. My pitchers had found out that it was better to fool the hitter at the plate, and not worry about catching men off bases. They might throw over to first three or four times to keep the runner on, but then they'd turn and whistle that ball in there.

We had a very hard time getting into that World Series in the first place. Somebody figured out that the Yankees had a total of seventy-one injuries and ailments that kept men from playing at different times during the 1949 season.

We started out pretty good, and Joe McCarthy's Red Sox started slow. But he got them coming along, and they were gaining on us near the end of June, when we went to play them a three-game series in Boston. And they were a team that would hardly ever lose at home. They would on the road, but very seldom at home.

Well, Mr. DiMaggio had just got well enough to play for us, and he hit four home runs in the three games and we swept the series. The greatest thing about it was the way it pepped up our ballplayers. They said, "Now we've got this wonderful man back, and he's going to be the leader for us."

They believed he was the best man on the club, and I found out for myself that he was. In the outfield he was like a captain. I never had to shift my outfielders with DiMaggio in center. If he went over toward right-center, the left fielder and right fielder would shift with him. If he moved to left-center, they'd move that way.

It was amazing to see him come charging in and catch balls that other outfielders would play on one hop. He'd get a tremendous jump, and he just seemed to be going where the ball was—it looked like he had a radar beam that he'd follow.

Joe would run out to his position at the start of an inning, and run back in when it was over. And he'd smoke a cigarette, maybe, between innings—but always underneath the stand; never in public.

As a right-handed hitter his home park was against him, but he did a great job at the plate anyhow. Yankee Stadium is so deep in left-center, where his power was, that they made many a terrific catch off him out there. But he'd just go along as if nothing had happened. He'd never give the other team the satisfaction of showing that it bothered him. He knew other hits would come, the way he could swing that bat.

That 1949 race went right down to the end of the schedule. The Red Sox began catching up to us again, and finally went ahead of us. With two games to go they had a one-game lead.

We were playing them those last two games at Yankee Stadium. So we were then at the point where Stengel had to platoon himself out of a job or platoon himself in.

They took a 4-0 lead in the first game, but we tied the score and then won it on Lindell's homer in the eighth inning, 5-4. In the last game we got the lead and just held it to win, 5-3.

The minute the game was over, my friend Joe McCarthy, the Boston manager, showed the kind of gentleman he was. He shook my hand, and I said, "Well, Joe, you've won so many of them, maybe it's all right for me to win this one." And he said, "Yes, everything is fine and dandy, and I want to congratulate you."

I'd won pennants in the minor leagues, but this was my first as a major-league manager. And it was the best pennant I ever won.

20

One of the new things I did on the Yankees was to start an instructional school for some of the young ballplayers in our organization. We'd hold it before the regular spring training. The background of that school went back a long way. When I was managing in the minor leagues and in the National League, I used to go out during the off season in Glendale and see if I couldn't pick up a ballplayer or two. I'd go to the Griffith Park recreation center and work with kids.

I brought Bill Knickerbocker, an infielder, up to Toledo with me, and he went on and played eleven years in the American League. Then I brought Raoul Dedeaux, a shortstop, to Brooklyn with me, but he injured his spine and became a baseball coach at Southern California. Several years ago he moved up to head coach, and he has won four district championships and two national college championships. He says he uses the Stengel system.

Later on when I was managing Boston I worked some with Ralph Kiner and Gus Zernial, but I never got to sign them to contracts. And after I broke my leg at Boston in 1943 I had to cut down. I couldn't go out and hit fungos to the boys, and work with them on infield and outfield play. But I still did some scouting on the playgrounds during the wintertime.

With the Yankees my idea was that by having an instructional school we might be able to advance some of the younger players faster. Anybody that was red-hot at the school stayed on during spring training and had a chance to beat somebody out of a job that was on the regular roster.

I started the school in 1950, after my first year as the Yankee manager, because I could see we had a lot of older men that were nearing the end of their careers. I had all my coaches as instructors. Turner would take care of the pitchers, Dickey took care of the catchers and I had Crosetti to take care of the infielders. I generally handled the outfielders myself, with some help from Johnny Neun, who was in the Yankee organization. He'd been a manager and a first baseman, and I would put him in charge of the first basemen. Another man in the organization I brought down was Bill Skiff. He could help out in teaching both the catchers and the outfielders.

Then we'd also have the men come down that were going to manage clubs in our farm system that year. A man that had been a catcher, say, might be weak on shortstop and second base, and how to make the double play. And he could get an insight on that by listening to the coaches at the instructional school. We'd tell those managers to walk around and see if they couldn't find out some things they didn't know about different branches of play.

Our first instructional school in February 1950 only ran a very short time. There was a rule then that you

couldn't start spring training before March first. Some
people claimed we were breaking the rule, and we had to
close down our school.

In the regular season that year the Yankees again
weren't favored to win. In the baseball writers' poll 116
out of 194 picked the Red Sox, and only 38 voted for us.
Detroit was picked for third place, but it was Detroit
that ended up giving us the biggest battle. They were
leading the league in September, but we finally won out
by three games.

First base was one of the positions that began to change
on the Yankees in 1950. Henrich was handicapped se-
verely by his bad knee and was out most of the season, so
I used Joe Collins and Johnny Mize and Johnny Hopp.

It irritated some of Henrich's friends among the writers
when I put him on the disabled list for the World Series,
but it turned out that he was through. Doctors told him
over the winter that an operation might make his knee
better or it might make it worse, so he decided to quit
playing rather than take a chance on the operation.

In the 1950 World Series we played the Phillies and
won in four straight. These were all low-scoring games,
and their best one was pitched by Jim Konstanty. He
didn't throw hard, but he had beautiful control and believed in himself, and he stood out there and irritated
our hitters for nine whole innings. We finally beat him,
1-0, on a very cheap run. And on the strength of that
game I later bought Konstanty in 1954, and he helped me
win a pennant.

Those Phillies were called the Whiz Kids because
they were such a young team. Well, in the last game of
the Series our winning pitcher was Whitey Ford, who was
only twenty-one himself. He had a 5-0 lead in the ninth

inning, and the writers had their stories all written about how the Yankees' Whiz Kid had beaten the Philadelphia Whiz Kids.

But then an error was made and a couple of other men got on. A couple of runs scored, so I thought Ford might be getting tired and I put Allie Reynolds in to get the last out. The young man, Ford, had been throwing a lot of curves. And then this old man of thirty-five, Reynolds, came in, and he just threw lightning by a pinch hitter for the strikeout that ended the Series.

The next year, 1951, our instructional school began to produce. One of the players we had there was Mickey Mantle. He'd been in Class C ball at Joplin the year before. He was only nineteen, and he was a very timid boy. He came from a small town in Oklahoma.

There were five or six boys at the school that could run, and the coaches would clock them. And Mantle won all his races by so much, they thought at first that he must be jumping the gun. But he wasn't. He was just that fast.

He'd been a shortstop in the minor leagues and made numerous errors. Most of his errors were on throwing the ball—he had such a strong arm he'd overthrow the bases. We tried him at shortstop, but he wouldn't stand next to the other shortstop in practice and buck him for the job. He'd go twenty-five to fifty feet in back of him and play the balls from there.

Then we put Mantle in the outfield. He was going to play in center field in an exhibition game against the Cleveland club. He'd never used sun glasses before, but we gave him a pair and said, "Put these on."

Well, he thought he could play that sunny field without glasses. Out comes a high fly ball and hits him right on top of his head. It took a nice high bounce, and he just spun around and fell right flat. He wasn't hurt, but he was so embarrassed that he just lay there and covered his face. He didn't get up and come in. We had to go out there and get him.

He was a switch hitter, and pretty soon everybody wanted to know, "Which way does he bat best?" He's the only man up to the present time that could switch between right- and left-handed at the plate without a loss of power. Generally a man hits the ball far one way but doesn't hit for distance the other.

Mantle made the ball club that year, although at one point during the season we sent him down to the American Association for some more experience. Another man that came to the Yankees from that 1951 instructional school was Gil McDougald. He had a very peculiar batting stance. But he'd been a good hitter under Hornsby at Beaumont, and he looked like a man that could play the infield.

I had Billy Martin and Coleman for second base and Rizzuto for shortstop, so I put McDougald at third base. Later on he also played other positions. I won world championships with Gil McDougald at third base, I won them with McDougald at second base and I won them with McDougald at shortstop. So I'd have to say he was a very valuable man for me.

In that 1951 season we were in a pennant fight with the Cleveland team. We were all even with them on September seventeenth when we played them a game in Yankee Stadium. Lemon was pitching a wonderful game for them, and Lopat was out there for us giving their hitters five or six different motions and keeping them off stride. Lopat always was a jinx to that Cleveland club.

Well, we come down to the ninth inning with the score

1-1. It looks like whoever wins this game should go on and win the pennant, which is the way things worked out. We're at bat in the ninth, and with one out DiMaggio beats out an infield hit. Woodling singles him to third. Then they walk Bobby Brown intentionally to fill the bases and give themselves a force play at any base.

Now here comes one of the most beautifully executed plays I've ever seen. Rizzuto is at the plate. He's a pretty good bunter, and might be able to squeeze DiMaggio home with the winning run. But Lemon is a great pitcher at fielding his position, and so is Hegan, the catcher—they generally kept us from bunting too much.

Cleveland is ready for the squeeze. Rosen, the third baseman, says to DiMaggio off third base, "I think this man is going to bunt." DiMaggio says, "It wouldn't surprise me," and turns away with that cold stare he has.

Lemon pitches a strike to Rizzuto. Then he winds up again, and as he winds up he's watching to see if DiMaggio starts breaking for home. If DiMaggio does, then Lemon will pitch out so Rizzuto can't bunt, and DiMaggio will be tagged at the plate.

But good old Joe just stands there till the moment Lemon opens his fingers to release the ball, and then he makes his break. The pitch is inside, which makes it tough for Rizzuto to bunt down the first-base line, away from a right-handed pitcher, but he lays it down there anyhow.

The bunt was so perfect and DiMaggio had such a big jump that the Cleveland catcher just turned and started walking off the field before Joe even crossed the plate. Lemon ran over and picked up the ball, and when he saw it was impossible to make a play, he tried to throw the ball over the grandstand.

In the 1951 World Series we played the Giants.

Durocher was the manager, and he brought them out full of cocaine. They gave us the rush act at first. They had Eddie Stanky playing second base, and he was a little stunty, like he always was in trying to win a game. He'd reach out and give a man a little pinch when he went by him at second. At the plate he'd try to get hit with pitched balls, and he'd duck his knees to get the umpire to call balls on low pitches.

Then in the fifth inning of the third game he kicked the ball out of Rizzuto's hand sliding into second. They scored five runs that inning and won the game, 6-2, to go ahead in the Series. But I'm not saying Stanky handicapped us, because when he pulled that on Rizzuto, DiMaggio got irritated, and so did some of the other players, and that put us in high gear for the rest of the Series. We took the last three games to win it.

We had one big break. It rained between the third and fourth games, when we were down two games to one, and that gave me an extra day of rest for my pitching staff, which I needed.

We also had a bad break. In the second game, which was played in Yankee Stadium, a ball was hit between DiMaggio in center field and Mantle in right. They both ran over for it, and all of a sudden Mantle's knee gave out from under him. He was out the rest of the Series, and that was the start of the leg trouble that's been a big problem at times in his baseball career.

We needed new men like Mantle for the years ahead, because the great players I started out with in New York were beginning to give out. Keller was gone. Henrich had retired after 1950. And then DiMaggio retired after 1951. He decided he was past his prime. He said, "I've never been booed in New York, and I don't want to be."

So we had to try and keep bringing up new talent.
It wasn't easy to find, what with the Korean War drafting
young men, the professional football teams all looking for
athletes, and some of the baseball clubs paying boys big
bonuses to sign. The question was: Could we go on winning while we were rebuilding?

21

✂ Everybody knows we had a lot of playing talent during the years I was managing the Yankees, but a lot of people don't realize how fast the talent kept wearing out. By the time of the 1952 World Series, we had only two of the regulars that had started my first World Series for me in 1949—Berra and Rizzuto. The others were all traded or retired or in the military service.

One of our biggest problems in 1952 was to replace DiMaggio in center field. We didn't think we could move Mantle over there from right field because he was handicapped in covering ground with his knee that he'd hurt in the 1951 World Series. And it also turned out that he'd had osteomyelitis in one leg, which is a very serious thing.

That kept him out of the draft. He was examined three times in different cities and turned down. This bothered him, because people would yell from the stands and ask him why he wasn't in the Army. On the field he could run fast and everything.

But for three or four years Mantle couldn't turn and cut quick because of that knee. He could only run in a straight line. On the bases he'd have to swing wide around first instead of cutting sharp toward second. And in the outfield he was very troubled on balls hit over his head. Later on he found a way where he could circle back better and overtake the baseball at times.

Another possibility for center field was Jackie Jensen. We had gotten him and Billy Martin from Oakland in 1950. But we decided that Jensen's best position was right field, where we already had Mantle. So in May of 1952 we gave up Jensen to get Irv Noren, a center fielder with the Washington club.

Noren had been sensational playing against us, but after we got him, he misjudged the first ball that was hit to him in center field. And we found out that he also had had knee trouble. So it ended up that Mantle became the center-fielder after all, while Noren was used mostly in left field. Next to Woodling, he did the best defensive work for me there—he was a very good thrower.

Well, we were in another hot pennant fight with Cleveland that season, and there was one point in September when it looked like we weren't going to win our fourth straight. We got in a slump, and in Philadelphia we lost a game I never expected to lose. In the clubhouse afterward I kept myself from handing out any comments, as when you're burned up, it's generally better to talk to your ballplayers the next day.

And the men commenced to get cans of beer in the clubhouse, and instead of walking over and dropping them in the trash can when they finished, they'd let them fly. It wasn't a very large trash can, and they'd miss, and the empty cans of beer would bounce around and go ting-a-ling, ting-a-ling. There were so many ting-a-lings that it began to get my goat. It looked to me like they were kidding around too much and not taking this slump seriously. And I could see it was getting on one of the pitcher's nerves, too.

But I got out of there without saying anything. Then in the dining car to Washington they started this game called Twenty Questions. The game got going good, and they were laughing and joking, and it wasn't so funny to me. I jumped up and asked for their attention. I asked if they realized that hardly a one of them had earned his salary that day. I told them it wasn't any laughing matter, and they didn't know what their salary would be for the following year or where they'd be playing, as it looked like this season was going to be a failure. I gave them as good a jacking up as I could, and it may have helped to keep them bearing down hard the rest of the year.

We won the pennant by two games over Cleveland, and in the 1952 World Series we played Brooklyn. We got down to the seventh inning of the seventh game with a 4-2 lead, and then they filled the bases with two out and Jackie Robinson at bat.

Bob Kuzava came in to pitch for us. You weren't supposed to be able to pitch left-handers against those Brooklyn right-handed hitters, especially in Ebbets Field, but Kuzava made Robinson pop this high infield fly. It went so high it looked like it would go over the Washington Monument if you were in Washington. And while it was up in the air, each player looked at the others and said, "I don't want it, you take it." It was like that ball was a bomb that nobody wanted to handle.

At second base we had Billy Martin, who had taken over the position when Gerry Coleman was called back into the military service on account of the Korean War. This pop fly wasn't Martin's ball, but he started running for it. He ran right up near home plate and made a diving grab of the ball four inches from his knees. If that ball hadn't been caught, all the men on the bases would have scored, because everybody was running, and Robinson would have gotten around maybe to third.

In 1953 Martin was a World Series hero against Brooklyn again with twelve hits in twenty-four times at bat. Later on, of course, he got traded away in 1957. This was after some sort of fight broke out at the Copacabana night club when some of our players and their wives had a party there to celebrate Martin's birthday. If I ever go into the restaurant business, I think I'll invite some ballplayers and their wives to come there at night, because the Copacabana got the most publicity out of that I ever saw.

I don't know anything about the fight. I didn't see it. But the bad part was that we had a game the next day. Originally it was to be an off day, but then we had to make up a game that had been rained out. Martin's group had made their plans for that night in advance, and they went ahead with the party anyway. They didn't come and ask me if they could. If I'd said yes, it would have been all right. But when you don't get permission from the manager, then you're going at your own risk.

The owners and Mr. Weiss didn't like that at all, and didn't think the manager was handling his players right. Some fines were made. I don't know the exact amount, because it was done by the office. And about a month afterward Billy Martin was traded to Kansas City.

Now here's the situation with Martin. He was a young man that came out of a neighborhood, which we have in every city, which they try to watch. He'd had a stepfather.

Martin was a small man. He thought he could whip anybody. And when anybody tells you Martin can't fight, that's a big joke. Martin can fight good.

He gave me a lot of spirit and everything else. Sometimes you have to have a noisy man on the team. You can have too many quiet players, and you need a man to jack them up. Martin could yell and yell at the other side, and he was a game player. And Martin is a skilled player. He knows all the plays, knows what's coming up, and he can catch the signs.

There was one thing that no doubt got him in a little bad with our ball club. He could not see the ideas of some of the men that were up in the front office. He was a man that was better for the players or better for the manager—if you could handle him. I could handle Billy Martin.

Did I approve of trading him? Well, the office had been after me three or four times to get rid of him. But I gave in only when they arranged to get me a left-handed hitter, Harry Simpson, who I thought would help us in Yankee Stadium. And we had Bobby Richardson coming along to play second base for us. As it worked out, Simpson didn't help us much. Anyway, I will have to say that there were very rare occasions on that ball club that they could slip around and get rid of a player if I didn't approve of the deal.

Getting back to 1953, we set a record by winning our fifth straight pennant and world championship that year. Then in 1954 we no doubt got a little careless. Everybody was saying, "Why would you change now?" Well, we didn't win the pennant that year, and this was a very big shock to the manager and the players, but we didn't really get off the beam. We won 103 games that year, which was the most we won while I was managing the Yankees. But

Cleveland won 111 games for a new American League record.

The Cleveland managing under Al Lopez was very good. His coaching was good. I knew the abilities of him and some of his men from when they worked under me as players in the National League. And they had very good pitching.

I would say that Early Wynn had the faculty of frightening you. He can throw a ball just around the shoulders, and the players are afraid not to swing when he gets two strikes on them. He had four or five different pitches, and he's a mean, domineering man in the box.

Bob Lemon had a fine sinker. His stuff was better when he didn't throw the ball too hard. The ball would dip more before it got to the plate. It would go in different directions.

Then they had Mike Garcia, and he did a pretty good job with his arm. Those three pitchers had ability and were daring. They would say, "Well, you're not going to knock us apart." And we only did on a few occasions.

But that season did not break our team, as was proven the next year when we came back to win out over Cleveland. Their biggest success in 1954 had been against the second-division clubs—they only broke even for the season against us and the White Sox. In 1955 the lower teams started saving up their best pitchers for Cleveland, the way they'd been doing for us, and that may have made some of the difference.

We started out as though we were very easily going to win the 1955 World Series too, because we went out ahead of Brooklyn by two games. Then they put in a very good left-handed pitcher, Podres, and he came up with a pitch that shocked my hitters. He took some of the speed off the ball, which you'd call a change-up. It was a pull-the-string-ball, and we couldn't detect it, because he had it down in great style.

We thought he couldn't go nine innings—he hadn't pitched a complete game since July. So we kept waiting him out, but he would pull the string on the ball and get it over. And that made him last more innings, because he didn't really have to extend himself. So he beat us twice, and Brooklyn won the World Series for the first time.

It went seven games, and we had one good chance in the last game, which Podres pitched. Berra came up to the plate in the sixth inning with a man on first and a man on second. We were behind, 2-0, and I had Berra hit away. Other teams always play Berra to pull to right, but the Brooklyn left fielder, Amoros, moved even farther around toward right than is usually done. Well, Podres pitched Berra outside, and the ball had a little too much speed for Berra to pull it, so he went with the pitch and hit the ball down the left-field line. I thought Amoros had shifted too far to get it, but he ran all the way over and made an amazing catch. And the game ended up at 2-0.

After the World Series the Yankees made a tour of Japan. Things were much different than when I went there on a barnstorming trip after the 1922 season. Instead of small wooden ball parks, they now had big stadiums. We would fill the stadiums, and there would be enormous crowds to see us in the street parades we had before the games.

I would be in the number one car in these parades. Many of the Japanese kids spoke some English, and they'd see me there with my gray hair. And I'd hear them saying to each other, "There's big shot. Old man is big shot."

One thing we did on that trip was to experiment with

McDougald as a shortstop. Rizzuto had dropped out after 1954, and we'd tried different men at the position, and I thought this was a good time to find out if McDougald could play short. So we used him there on the trip, and the next year he became an outstanding shortstop and made some very beautiful plays.

We won another pennant fairly easily in 1956 and beat Brooklyn in a seven-game World Series, with Larsen pitching his perfect game. Mantle had his first tremendous year. He led the league in four major departments—batting average (.353), home runs (52), runs batted in (130) and runs scored (132).

We now had a team that'd been rebuilt almost completely. And most of it had had to come from our farm system and our instructional school. We did get some good men in trades, like Larsen and Turley from Baltimore after the 1954 season, but as we went on winning championships, numerous owners got to saying, "Don't deal with the Yankees. Let's just trade with each other."

From our instructional school we got Bob Grim in 1954; he had been pitching for a Class A team and then gone into the military service, and he won twenty games his first year. We brought up Johnny Kucks in 1955, and he won eighteen games in 1956. We put Jackie Jensen and Billy Martin through the school, and a number of others.

In 1954 we brought up Bill Skowron, and he became an amazing man at first base, although he'd had injury trouble. In 1955 we came up with another amazing man, Elston Howard. He had started out as a right fielder in the minor leagues, and had also been a catcher. Because we had Hank Bauer, I could not go along with Mr. Howard in right field. I had to make him a left fielder at the beginning. Then we worked him back into becoming a catcher.

He has a beautiful throwing arm—he throws a very light ball to second base that is easy for the infielders to handle. And Howard became a man I could platoon as an out-fielder or as a catcher, and also as a first baseman if Skowron was hurt.

Elston Howard was the first Negro player on the Yan-kees. He had a wonderful faculty of getting along with his teammates. He was a man that joined the ball club and never gave an official, never gave a manager, never gave anybody connected with the ball club any trouble of any kind.

In 1957 we got two more new men who advanced to regular positions on the Yankees. One was Bobby Richard-son, a second baseman, and the other was Tony Kubek. He was a shortstop, but I used him quite a bit at other positions in the infield and the outfield. He could do a splendid job in the outfield. He'd get a good start on the ball and had a good throwing arm. Once when Mantle's legs got hurt, Kubek was one of the few men that could go in and play center field.

He was far from being a great shortstop when he first came up, in my personal opinion. I'd had Eddie Miller at Boston, I'd had Rizzuto and McDougald on the Yankees —I'd had some splendid shortstops. They were experi-enced and knew how to make the plays.

A shortstop is the same thing as a quarterback out there. He's got to go and back up every play; he's got to watch every base; he's got to go out and take relays. Any place where the ball is hit, he's got to have a spot he goes to. He has to go all over the ball park. And Kubek had a lot to learn. He still was not a great shortstop when I left the Yankees, but he had become a good one, and he's kept on getting better.

Well, we won another pennant there in 1957, although we lost a seven-game World Series to Milwaukee. When you can keep on winning like that when you're blending in new men, a club is being run all right on the ball field. It's being run all right in the office. But although I didn't know it yet, there was trouble just ahead. Things in the office were about to change.

22

✂ Toward the end of the 1958 season there was a lot of talk that I was through with the Yankees. It was being said that either I wouldn't sign up again when my contract expired in October, or the club wouldn't sign me. I don't know where all that gossip started. It wasn't put out by me. It might have come from somebody in the office, because the situation there was commencing to change.

When we lost three of the first four games in the World Series that year to the Milwaukee team, which had beaten us in 1957, numerous people were surer than ever that I would leave. Spahn was an amazing pitcher for Milwaukee in that series, the way his roommate Burdette had been the year before, which I'll say more about a little later.

Anyhow, everybody thought we were going to take the loser's share again. Then when things turned around, with us sweeping the last three games to come out on top, people natually were in sympathy with the manager to stay on. I've been told since that Mr. Topping would have been willing to have me leave anyway, but Mr.

Webb and Mr. Weiss were against it. And I signed another two-year contract.

Well, maybe we were a little too enthusiastic after coming back and winning three straight games over that great Milwaukee team, with men like Aaron in their line-up. I didn't know we were headed for the only really bad season the players had, and possibly myself, in my twelve years with the Yankees. We'd lost back in 1954 despite 103 victories because somebody else—Cleveland—won 111 games. In 1959 we didn't win but seventy-nine games and we finished a bad third, fifteen games behind Al Lopez and the White Sox.

The White Sox had been giving us competition for six or seven years. They began picking up a number of fast men under Frank Lane as general manager. In Chicago, and eventually around the league, they became known as the "Go Go Go Sox."

They were not a good hitting team, so they made their living running bases. They'd keep going for extra bases when you weren't expecting it. It was what you'd call a surprise or shock play. And on these shock plays you'd hurry the throw and overthrow first base, overthrow third base. They'd just keep on going, and maybe score two or three runs on an infield ball that should have been a double play. They did it first with Paul Richards as manager, and then Al Lopez came there with his coaches from Cleveland and put in the same kind of system.

They had some outstanding ballplayers. Fox played a good game in the field at second base, and he'd stand up at the plate and barber and keep the boys irritated. And he'd even walk by and step on the resin bag for our bats, and make the resin run out.

Aparicio was the Rizzuto type of shortstop. He could go clear to third base to catch balls, go to second and catch them, go over his head and catch a fly ball. He could make a double play. And he hit better in the major leagues than he did in the minor leagues. He's a dangerous man to put on first base, because he bothers the pitcher. A little hit and he may go to third base on it, or he'll go down to second and steal. And he'll go a month without being thrown out, which is when a man becomes valuable as a base stealer.

Well, we were in that pennant fight until August. And then we went up to Boston—a club that hadn't given us any trouble for several years—and lost five straight games. After that we never did get back in the race.

This bad 1959 season was an emergency to our owners. They thought the manager was slipping. They thought the coaches were slipping. They thought the players were slipping.

But maybe those people in the front office didn't have such a good year themselves. They decided to do without my instructional school, which had been sending up young ballplayers almost every season—I notice they went back to it in 1961. And they also decided to get tough about salaries, even though we'd just won a world championship. They changed that too in 1961—just about all the players were smiling when they left the owners or the business manager after signing their contracts.

But back there in 1959 it was like it had been after we won the 1916 pennant when I was playing for Brooklyn. The owner says, "I won't keep you here unless you sign up for what I want to pay you. I'll trade you." Now that's a bad thing. You ought to get rid of a man when he shows no spirit. And his spirit shouldn't come from the salary.

Even if a club hasn't made money the previous season, the owner should always be able to raise a man who deserves it by two thousand or four thousand.

Well, when you go into spring training the way we did in 1959, with several men still unsigned, and several others who have signed contracts but are dissatisfied, that can be a pretty hard thing for a manager. Take Mantle. Since he became a star, he'd never once gone to spring training without some hard feeling over his contract negotiations. And then I'd be told, "Why don't you make the man mind you?" Well, the owners could try it themselves, and then they might find out they're not so bright either, except that they own the man's contract.

But regardless of who was to blame—and maybe it was all of us—I can tell you what was wrong with the 1959 Yankee club on the field. First of all, the runs-batted-in were off, except for Hector Lopez, who we got in a trade with Kansas City, and Elston Howard, who had been a valuable man for me for several years. The only .300 hitter on the team was Richardson (.301), and he doesn't hit for distance or drive in many runs.

Mantle had seventy-five runs batted in and thirty-one home runs in 1959, which was just a fair year for him. Here's something about Mantle that not many people know. After leading the league in four things in 1956 and hitting .365 in 1957, he tore a ligament in his right shoulder in the '57 World Series against Milwaukee. It happened when he was pulling out from under Schoendienst on an attempted pick-off play at second base. This bad shoulder hampered him in his throwing for the next couple of years, and it also handicapped him at the plate when he was batting left-handed, which he does most of the time. Whenever he missed on a hard swing it would tear at his shoulder. The result was that he developed a hitch in his swing. He became too much of a lift hitter. His swing wasn't level enough.

Our defense also was somewhat off in 1959, mostly because of inexperience in the infield, and the pitching slipped some too. Art Ditmar had his best year for me, but one of my top men, Whitey Ford, had some arm trouble. He had what would be a good year for most men, but it wasn't up to his best.

But the big disappointment was Bob Turley. He's a fine, good-looking boy, and a very bright man—very intellectual. He came to us from Baltimore with Don Larsen in 1955, and he wasn't a great pitcher at first. But he got to where he could beat the good clubs, and in 1958 he became a man like Allie Reynolds used to be, that could win games both starting and in relief.

He won twenty-one games and lost only seven during the season that year, and did a great job in the World Series. But in 1959 he dropped down to eight and eleven. There was nothing wrong with his arm or his willingness to work. He just couldn't win.

Well, as I told you, the Yankee ownership got very disturbed over the way things were going that year. They would have liked to get rid of a lot of people, including the manager and most of the coaches. But I was signed through 1960. In the end the only man to lose his job was Jim Turner, the pitching coach.

Although I didn't choose my own coaches when I first came to the Yankees, I thought that most of the time their work was very good. I gave them complete authority to make the players carry out their orders, and if they didn't do it, it wasn't because the manager didn't back them up. Of course, a coach can have an off year, just the same as a ballplayer. But over the twelve years, I thought that on the average the coaches did their jobs as well as the players, and possibly a little better.

I must have been satisfied with the way they instructed the players and handled their other duties, because look at how long they stayed. We started out with just three full-time coaches—Crosetti, Dickey and Turner. Crosetti is still there. Dickey lasted until 1958, when his doctors make him quit because of his health. Then Ralph Houk, a bullpen catcher who had gone to Denver as a manager in the meantime, came back to replace him.

Now here's the situation on Turner. He was supposed to instruct the pitchers and keep them in shape, and in consultation with me he'd give the orders to the bullpen during games. We worked a telephone system from the bench, Turner and I. I would tell him who should go in the bullpen and who should warm up, and he'd get right on the phone.

We'd have our relief pitchers picked before the game, but we might change our minds in the seventh, eighth and ninth innings. I'd say, "Get a pitcher ready down there," and sometimes he might ask if somebody else would be all right instead of the pitcher we'd originally planned.

And things went along pretty well for a number of years, but in 1959 there were complaints about the way our pitching dropped off—especially Turley. Sometimes he'd have control trouble, and he wouldn't always throw as hard as he can. It got to where it looked like he was experimenting on all the hitters with slow stuff and junk.

So everybody commenced saying, "He's being taught wrong by that pitching coach." And they blamed the manager considerably too. Of course, we got Turley to go back to his fast ball and he kept on losing anyway, but that was overlooked. And Mr. Turner lost his job, but evidently not his reputation, as he was hired as the Cincinnati pitching coach in 1961 after running the Nashville ball club in 1960.

For the Yankees in 1960 the question was whether we could do a comeback. And we did. We again became a team that could win in our own ball park, where we play half our games. We had some trouble there in 1959, but in 1960 we could win at Yankee Stadium. We could play extra-inning games and win; we could play doubleheaders and win.

We had competition from the White Sox again, but even more from the Baltimore club. Paul Richards, the manager that started building up the White Sox, had taken over Baltimore in 1955. He went into a big spending spree and picked up a lot of recruits. He was successful with his pitchers, and when you pick up a pitching staff, you're getting near the first division.

Richards is general manager of the new Houston club in the National League now. Anyhow, all the time he was at Baltimore his team played like a first-division club, whether they finished there or not. They were young and he kept them hustling. And by 1960 he had a strong infield along with a good pitching staff.

In September the Baltimore team was leading the league. Then they came into Yankee Stadium to play us a four-game series. Some of the business managers around the league had the idea that the Yankees were going dead. They said, "Baltimore will at least split even with them, or beat them. They flopped last year, they'll flop again."

And those young men from Baltimore came into Yankee Stadium all coked up. They seemed to think it was nothing to play the Yankees. But we didn't flop again. I'm not going to say we annihilated them, but we got to their best pitchers and won all four games. That was part of a fifteen-game winning streak we had there at the end of the 1960 season, and it ended up that we won the pennant by eight games.

The biggest difference over 1959 was made by four men. Roger Maris had the greatest first half of the season for us you ever saw. In spite of getting hurt during the second half, he led the league for the year in runs batted in with 112, and in home runs Mantle just barely caught him, with forty to Maris's thirty-nine. And Maris could throw and make sensational catches in right field.

Cletis Boyer did an amazing job at third base fielding. He didn't miss grounders, had an accurate arm and would sometimes hit home runs. Then in the pitching department we added two important men during the season. One was Luis Arroyo, an older pitcher, and the other was a young man, Bill Stafford.

How did we get those four men? Well, Boyer and Stafford came out of our own farm system. Boyer had been with us part of 1959. We didn't bring Stafford up until near the end of 1960; if we'd had an instructional school that year, I'm sure I'd have brought him up at the very start.

Arroyo was a man Mr. Weiss got for me from the International League. I'd mentioned before that I'd like to get him, but a couple of the newer men in the Yankee office had seen Arroyo in the National League, and they didn't think much of his pitching. Finally I said to Mr. Weiss, "I have to have an experienced man like that in this pennant race. We've done that before with Sain. We've done that with Konstanty. I need that man very badly." So Mr. Weiss went ahead and got me Arroyo. He was just what we needed as a relief pitcher at the end of 1960, and he helped the Yankees all season long in 1961.

Maris we got over the winter from Kansas City. I didn't know how good Maris was, as he hadn't played regular. He had a great reputation. He could run, he could bunt, he could hit a ball hard. But the year before he had had appendicitis, and didn't have a very good season.

Well, in December of 1959 we heard that Kansas City was thinking about trading Maris. I said to Mr. Weiss, "You keep kicking that we need an outfielder that can drive in runs and hit home runs in Yankee Stadium, you could make a deal for this man." And Mr. Weiss did the big job. He had to give up a number of players—Siebern, Bauer, Larsen and Throneberry—to get me the man that was to give us our biggest inspiration for the first half of 1960.

Let's talk a minute about George Weiss, a man I've known in baseball since 1925. When I first came to the Yankees he was my boss. The owners gave him full authority. I'd say he held it until the last two or three years. Then I could see that factions were developing in the office. Now there were some good men in that office—I don't care what faction they were working for. But the teamwork up there was not so good.

The thing was that the owners felt they knew the baseball business now, after being in it a number of years. They possibly thought, "I'm on league committees. I am now where I know what ought to be done. I know where we ought to have different men in the office. I know where new players ought to be blended into the ball club."

One of the owners, Mr. Topping, now wanted to *be* the president of the club, not just to have the title. So people in the office had to be on that side of the fence or else they were going to get the moving van—which is, they put you in a moving van and move you away.

And Mr. Weiss was on the way out—along with myself.

23

✂ The last month and a half of the 1960 season I could tell that I was through as manager of the Yankees. The attitude of people in the office that I knew and liked was different. They knew that things were going to change.

I said to Mr. Weiss near the end of the season, "You're not running this club the way you were before, or I don't hear everything. I believe that this club is being run better on the field now than it is in the office."

And he dropped his head and said, "I'm afraid you're right."

A few things went wrong in the 1960 World Series against Pittsburgh, and we lost to them in seven games. But if we'd been a little luckier and won, it wouldn't have made any difference about whether I was going to stay on.

Back in New York after the Series, one of the two owners, Mr. Webb, phoned me and said he wanted to see me, as he had to leave for a meeting on the West Coast. So I went down from my apartment in the Essex House to his suite at the Waldorf-Astoria. Mr. Topping, the other owner, was there too.

I was pretty sure before I got there what was going to happen. There wasn't any big conversation. Nobody said, "You did a good job this year. Look at the attendance we had on the road and at home. The team hasn't gotten away from you, except in the eighth and ninth innings of the last World Series game."

There was no contract out on the table for me to sign, the way there had been all the other times. When you don't see the contract, you know the ball is there. And I knew it was there and had been there. I could tell from the smiles on the owners' faces. And I told them they didn't have to tell me what the score was.

They would have liked to announce right afterward that I was leaving the Yankees, but I insisted that it be done at a meeting of the writers and broadcasters, which was set up for Tuesday, October eighteenth. Mr. Topping told the press it was because of my age, which was seventy. A couple of weeks later the age program also caught up to Mr. Weiss, who is several years younger than I am.

Another thing Mr. Topping announced was that they were giving me a check for $160,000. He made it sound like it was some special gift from the owners. Actually, this was money that had been set aside for me over the twelve years as my share in the Yankees' profit-sharing pension plan. All full-time Yankee employees are in on this except for the ballplayers, who naturally have their own pension program. It was the success of our teams on the field that made the plan possible, not to mention the big profits that were earned by the owners themselves. The exact amount my share came to in the time I worked there was $158,747.25.

The ownership was always fair with me on salary. I

started off at $35,000 a year, then was raised to $50,000. The last six years it was $75,000. On top of that was the money that was credited to me in the profit-sharing pension plan, and there also was usually a World Series share. And I often got a bonus for a winning season.

So the last few years it generally all added up to around $100,000. The owners said they didn't think a manager should get any more than that. And I thought they were right.

I always signed two-year contracts. I asked once or twice for one-year contracts, but they always wanted to make it for two years. The last time I was glad I did sign up for two years. That was the only time I needed it.

If they'd offered me another contract there at the end of 1960, the money wouldn't have been any problem. But I'd have said, "First I want to ask you people a few things. Who's running the office now? Is everything changed around? Who makes the deals? Do I get to say yes? Are you going to put out more money for players? Are you going to allow me to have my instructional school again? I'm lost without it. I'm not getting to bring new players up, and I'm losing some of the ability of my coaches, because they don't get to instruct down there with me watching them."

But none of this came up, because they had their own plans made, and I wasn't part of them. That's all right. The ownership should plan ahead, and it can run a club any way it wants to. I have no grievance. The only thing I'd say is that those owners got to be too much like fans— one of them especially. They'd second-guess me to people, and I'd eventually hear about it. You shouldn't gossip like that about a man that's worked for you so many years, and had winning teams that made a lot of money for you.

I left them a ball club that was on top, and I don't see any reason why the Yankees shouldn't go on and win more pennants. I wish them every success. I wish success to the new manager, Ralph Houk. He's a man that has had to work hard to stay in baseball, because his skill was limited as a ballplayer. He had to find something else, and he's been very serious about it. He did a very good job of managing the Yankees to a pennant and world championship in 1961.

I told you that when Berra was catching practically all the games in my first few years with the Yankees, we would put an extra catcher out in the bullpen as an assistant coach to warm up the relief pitchers. The man that did that job at first was Charlie Silvera, and the next man was Houk. Houk later was put in charge of the farm team at Denver. Silvera also became a manager in the minor leagues, but he didn't have much luck.

When Dickey stopped coaching because of his health in 1958, Houk came up to the Yankees as a coach. He possibly was going to get hired away from Denver by some other club. Anyhow, our office wanted him to come up and take the place of Mr. Dickey, and I agreed to have him do it.

When the owners were talking about firing coaches in 1959, he's the one man they would sure keep. When I was out sick for a week or so early in the 1960 season Houk ran the club as acting manager, and it was my recommendation that he should run it. So when he became the manager in 1961, it wasn't any stranger coming in to take over the ball club. The players knew him. And the owners, I am positive, knew him, and had it arranged that he was to move up.

Now I'd like to talk about the Yankee ballplayers. I had

some great ones during my twelve years in New York. First I'm going to pick the top nine, and then I'll build it into an all-star squad of twenty-five. If I could have had all these men at the same time, there wouldn't have been very much for me to do as a manager. About the only thing they'd have needed would have been somebody to hit fungos to the infield and the outfield before the games.

I would say that DiMaggio, by all means, was the leading light. He could throw, he could go to his right, he could go to his left, he could come in on a ball, he could get a start on a ball back over his head. He played in a park that wasn't built for him as a right-handed batter, and they caught many well-hit balls off him, but he still was a terrific hitter. He knew how to run bases, knew how to execute every play in baseball, always knew what should be done at the proper time. So why does he need a manager?

I have Berra picked as number two. He was one of the three greatest catchers that's ever been in the American League—Mickey Cochrane and Bill Dickey were the two greatest. And he can also play left field and right field. He's a man that looks funny in a uniform, and maybe looks awkward and so forth. But he's actually quick, he's a terrific hitter and he's very hard for the other pitchers to fool.

Mantle is third, but he's a man that could still wind up being outstanding in more things than anybody else. Mantle had more ability than any player I ever had on that club. He can slug the ball right-handed or left-handed. He can run and overtake the ball in the outfield, and on the bases he's one of the fastest men that ever lived. He'll do everything a little better than the ordinary man.

Stengel's all-star Yankee squad

(1949-60)

Starting Pitchers	Vic Raschi Allie Reynolds Whitey Ford Ed Lopat Bob Turley
Relief Pitchers	Joe Page Johnny Sain Sal Maglie Luis Arroyo
Catchers	Yogi Berra Elston Howard
Infielders	Bill Skowron Gerry Coleman Phil Rizzuto Gil McDougald
Outfielders	Joe DiMaggio Mickey Mantle Roger Maris
Utility Infielders	Bobby Richardson Billy Martin
Utility Infielder-Outfielder	Tony Kubek
Utility First Baseman-Outfielder	Tommy Henrich
Utility Outfielders	Gene Woodling Hank Bauer Charlie Keller

There have been three things wrong with him. One, he had osteomyelitis. Two, they complained that he didn't tip his cap to the fans. Third, they said, "He gets mad at himself." But he never got mad at his own ballplayers. He's well liked by the ballplayers. So he's got a good disposition to be on a ball club.

Look what he's already done, despite being crippled up a lot of the time. Look what he may do in the future. He didn't turn thirty until October of 1961.

My fourth man is Allie Reynolds. He was my greatest pitcher to start and relieve. He could warm up quick and was amazing in relief, amazing starting. Vic Raschi is number five. He couldn't relieve like Reynolds, but he was my best starting pitcher. Those two men, Reynolds and Raschi, could befuddle the hitters more than anybody I ever had pitch for me.

Then I come to Whitey Ford. Ford is a young left-hander who has pitched when the Yankees possibly had inferior line-ups, yet has had a terrific earned-run average. He's been able to go in there and pitch to any type of hitter and stop any class of ball club. His greatest asset is that he can hold the runners on bases or pick them off. And he's a game little fellow and dosen't get nervous.

The seventh man is another pitcher, Ed Lopat. He started in baseball as a first baseman and had to learn to pitch. He mixed up the pitches, he used a lot of gyrations with his arm and his shoulders. He was a left-hander that could fool the right-handed hitters, like the ones they had at Cleveland. He had a good screw ball, but when they tried to go to right field with it, he'd switch over to his curve.

For number eight, I'd have to take Phil Rizzuto out of all the infielders I had. He could run, he could bunt, he could go to his right or go to his left for a ground ball, and he was tremendous at going back over his head for fly balls. The left fielders sometimes have trouble at Yankee Stadium, with the sun and the shadows coming down there. Rizzuto made it much easier for them, the way he could race out from shortstop and catch the short fly balls.

For my ninth man I'll take Gil McDougald, because he could do such a good job all around the infield—short, second or third. And he's been up there in runs-batted-in.

Then there were some great players I had past their prime, like Charlie Keller and Tommy Henrich and Johnny Mize. And Roger Maris started in very strong for me in 1960, but I only had him the one year. The next manager will see more of him. Maris was even greater in 1961. He tied Babe Ruth's record of sixty home runs in a 154-game season, and then set a new record of sixty-one for a 162-game schedule.

Now let's go on from there and draw up a twenty-five-man roster of Yankee stars. I'll begin with the pitchers. With the lively ball, you need both starting pitchers and relief pitchers. I'm going to pick five starters and four relievers.

I've already named four starters—Reynolds, Raschi, Ford and Lopat. For the fifth one I'm picking Turley. He was the only man I had after Reynolds that could start and finish games, and in 1958 he won twenty-one games in the American League. You can't laugh that off.

The best relief pitcher I ever had was Joe Page. He could get the fire out quick. He just came in and blasted the ball in there. Then I'll have to go with Johnny Sain. He had been a twenty-game winner in the National League. I saw him over there when he started. While he was near the end of his career when we got him in August 1951, he knew something about baseball—knew how to bat, how to field, how to catch you off bases, how to get out there and pitch and have control.

Next I'll go to Sal Maglie. I never saw a pitcher that could do more in tough competition than Maglie when he was a starter with the Giants and Brooklyn, and it was the same when we picked him up in September 1957 to pitch in relief for us.

And then there's Luis Arroyo. I just had him a short time in 1960, but he was a great man to put in there to stop the other club in the seventh, eighth and ninth innings. And he kept on going like that in 1961.

For catching, I'd say two men would be enough. I've given you Yogi Berra. The other catcher is Elston Howard. He can hit the ball for distance. And when you're playing a team like the White Sox that can go, go, go, what's wrong with having a catcher like Howard, that can throw, throw, throw?

In the infield I've mentioned Rizzuto, the shortstop, and also McDougald—I'd put him at third base. At second base I'll take Gerry Coleman. He could make a double play better than any second baseman I had. He could make double plays on left-handed hitters, which is much harder than on right-handed hitters, because the man that bats left has that extra start in getting down to first base.

My first baseman would be Bill Skowron. He can hit a ball a mile and knows how to play the bag. As utility infielders I'll pick two of my second basemen, Bobby Richardson and Billy Martin. Martin I've talked about at other times in this story. Richardson is a very good double-play man, and does other things too. Tony Kubek I'd put down as a utility infielder and outfielder. I could platoon him in left field, center field and right field, along with shortstop.

In the outfield we have DiMaggio, Mantle and Maris as the regulars, with some very good men in reserve. Henrich and Keller—even being crippled up when I had them, they could still play good. Henrich played first base for me more than he did the outfield, so I'm making him a utility first baseman and outfielder.

Then I'd have to add Gene Woodling and Hank Bauer. Woodling could stand up at the plate and battle the pitcher—get a hit or get a base on balls—and could play left field. And there was nothing wrong with Hank Bauer. He played in the big leagues a dozen years, was a good base runner and a good fielder, and could hit left-handers as well as anybody you ever saw.

So we had a lot of amazing ballplayers. But I'll have to admit that there were also some very good ones that got away from us.

24

✂ I would say when I was managing the Yankees we generally held onto our best talent. I'd be glad to have the owners or anybody else go back over all the trades that were made during the twelve years, and see how many good players we lost. We only gave up about six or seven men that were really outstanding. And for some of them we got very good players in return. But no doubt about it, these were all men that proved after leaving the Yankees that they could play for any team in baseball.

The one that came back to haunt us the most probably was Lew Burdette. He used to be our property in the minor leagues, but we had to throw him in on a deal in August 1951 to get Johnny Sain from the Braves. We wanted a pitcher that could help us right away, and Sain did help us win several pennants.

Then in the 1957 World Series, Burdette came back to be the big man against us. Milwaukee beat us out in seven games, and he pitched three of their four victories. He was very good with a count of three-and-two, or two-and-two. He'd talk to the catcher, and kid the hitters and irritate them.

And he used a peculiar pitch. He could hit you on the handle of the bat or the end of it, or make you chase the ball. Well, we were kicking and crying that he was throwing spitballs, but I actually didn't kick too much myself. If a man can pull anything like that in a World Series, with six umpires around, then he's really doing a job.

If Burdette could cheat once in a while, he possibly would cheat. I think so many pitchers are stupid that they don't occasionally. I don't say that Burdette did throw the spitter. I don't say that he didn't

In May 1952, as I explained a while back, we gave away Jackie Jensen to get Irv Noren from Washington. We were hoping Noren could become our center-fielder, but left field turned out to be his best position for us. Jensen went on from Washington to Boston and became a very valuable player in right field, with his hitting ability and his runs-batted-in.

The next deal we lost out on was made in December 1953. We sent Vic Power to the Athletics in a trade that involved a number of players. The most important men we got in exchange were Harry Byrd and Eddie Robinson. We had to rebuild our pitching staff, because Raschi, Reynolds, and Lopat were getting near the end of the line. We thought Mr. Byrd could strengthen our staff, but he didn't live up to our expectations.

Robinson was an older player and he did help us at first base, where we had Skowron starting in. But Vic Power became an amazing man at first base. He's one of the greatest fielding first basemen in the American League, if not the greatest. He can play very deep and rob all the left-handed hitters. And he is a fairly good hitter himself.

Power was on his way up from our farm system when

we traded him, and so was Bill Virdon the next spring. We got Enos Slaughter from the Cardinals for Virdon and a couple of other rookies, and Slaughter with his experience was a useful man in the outfield for a time. But Virdon was a fine young outfielder. He had a long career ahead of him, and still does. He went from the Cardinals to Pittsburgh, and his fielding and hitting murdered us in the 1960 World Series.

In December 1954, in a very big trade with Baltimore that brought us Turley and Larsen, we had to give up men like Gene Woodling and Gus Triandos. Woodling had played good ball for us—he was on five world-championship teams—and he kept on doing it for the Orioles and other clubs.

Triandos wouldn't have got to catch much for the Yankees, with Yogi Berra there, but he developed into a fine catcher and a slugger type of hitter with the Orioles. And we let another catcher go in that deal—Hal Smith— who came back to hurt us in the 1960 World Series. He was with Pittsburgh by then, and in the eighth inning of the last game he came up as a pinch hitter with two men on base and hit a home run.

Then there's Woody Held. We sent him with Billy Martin and some others to Kansas City in 1957 and got several men in return. The one we expected the most of was Harry Simpson, and I'll have to say he was disappointing. We also got Ryne Duren in the deal, and he did a good job as a relief pitcher for a year or two, with a sensational strikeout record.

But we made a mistake in getting rid of Woody Held. He showed he could hit a ball a tremendous distance and be great at driving in runs. He had a wonderful arm and could play either infield or outfield. As an infielder, his arm was so terrific that he could boot the ball and still throw out the runner unless the runner was exceptionally fast.

And those are some of the best ballplayers that got away from the Yankees under me.

When I left the Yankees myself at the end of 1960, a lot of people said I wouldn't know what to do with myself outside of baseball. I don't have any real hobbies. So I seemed to put most all my time in on baseball. I'd stay up nights thinking or talking about it, and then I'd always get out to the ball park early the next day.

Why shouldn't a man go out early if he's interested in baseball? I noticed that John Mize always did. He knew every batting average. I could say to him, "What did so-and-so do yesterday?"—meaning a man on the team that was coming into Yankee Stadium that day. Whether it would be the Baltimore team or the Chicago team, he would know every good hitter in that line-up and how many hits he got. He'd been a great hitter himself, and led leagues or come close to leading them. And he knew what eveybody had got—a home run, triple or double. He had those things down, and he gave them to me right fast.

Yogi Berra was another man that came into the clubhouse early. I don't want to take anything away from him, because nobody can, but I think one reason he came out there was that then his darling little wife would get to take care of the children. The kids are grabbing hold of Pop all the time, so he comes out where he can sit in the clubhouse and listen to what goes on. And Berra was pretty well up on what happened to other players in the league.

So that's one thing about going out to the ball park

early if you're the manager. You get to see which ballplayers come in before they have to. The second thing is to find out, if you can, how many of them are crippled up. On the Yankees they would try to give you a typewritten doctor's report after the game or the next day. But if you go out in the morning you also can go into the training room and ask, "Has anybody been in for a rub?"

The man that's very ambitious comes out and gets a rub early. A trainer shouldn't have to rub twenty-five players every day. But if you have two or three trainers, some of the players like to come in for a rub during the practice hours, and maybe duck some of the hitting and fielding workouts.

The third reason why I came out early was that I could go over my plans for the day. I could think about who we had to pitch, and who was going to pitch for them. I could make plans to combat their pitcher, and decide what hitters to put in our line-up that day.

After the game I liked to see players get dressed and get out as quick as they could. Of course, some of the great players have trouble when they leave the park. People stand outside and want their autographs. And if a player is going to be irritated by this, maybe he's better off if he does sit around the clubhouse for an hour rather than go out and fight the crowd. Because it will only cause embarrassment for everybody.

But as a rule, you don't want players to hang around, because then they may start second-guessing themselves and each other. Before baseball got as well regulated as it is today, you'd sometimes have fights in the clubhouse between your own players. Well, if you're in a pennant race you don't want those fights. I've seen men get crippled up that way and handicap their play.

So after a game with the Yankees—especially a losing game—I'd always walk around the clubhouse to make sure that none of my players were about to get mad at one another. If a couple of them looked as though they were, I'd just stop a moment and give them a sharp look. That would be enough.

That's why I like to keep the writers out for a few minutes if I could—to give the players a chance to settle down. Some of the sports columnists today, and some of the people that write for magazines, aren't interested in what happens during the game. They'd rather get a scandal about how one player is mad at another, and is it going to hold back the team.

At one point the Yankees were allowing the news writers and photographers to come into the clubhouse right after a game. So I tried to fix it like they do at the World Series—within five minutes we let you come in. I couldn't do this on the road, but I did at home.

I always said when I was on the road that if I got beat, I wished they'd let me alone for a little while, as half the visiting clubhouses did not have a separate room for the manager. And when the writers would come in and ask questions about a man standing close enough that he could hear, like, "What was wrong with so-and-so today?"—then you'd get into a heated argument. And there were two or three occasions during my years as Yankee manager that I saw fit not to let the writers into the clubhouse.

I've had trouble with sports writers, photographers and broadcasters once in a while. They've done things I didn't like. The writers have been enthusiastic. They wrote what they thought was right. Maybe it was right.

But for the most part I've had splendid treatment from

the baseball writers. Some ballplayers think the writers are always out to knock them. That's silly. Four-fifths of them will write what is good about a player or a manager if they can.

Way back when Ring Lardner used to cover baseball, he'd tell me, "Just keep talking, and I'll get a story." And that's what I did as a manager. There was criticism from some of the people in the Yankee office that I sat around too much with the newspapermen. They forgot that the club got quite a bit of publicity from it.

I gave the writers a lot of time over the years, and it wasn't wasted. I have to speak very highly of the writers in New York City—men like Dan Parker and Joe Williams —that I've known from the days when I was managing Brooklyn, and the younger men that have come along. I have to thank the baseball writers all over the United States. They have been amazing and wonderful to me.

One thing that causes a lot of talk by some of the writers and the public is when they see a ballplayer drinking. Naturally these stories get exaggerated. At times you can have twenty-five men on a club, and twenty-three of them will take a drink. My last years on the Yankees it was much less than that. We had about ten men that didn't drink at all, ten that maybe would, and the rest in between.

Now I don't advocate drinking for ballplayers. But it's pretty hard to regulate the habits of players today, with the different hours of daytime and nighttime ball. The bad feature is if four or five men go out together. Say it's five men. Nobody wants to be cheap, so everybody buys a round of drinks. That's five drinks apiece. If each one buys two rounds, that's ten. If they buy three rounds, that's fifteen. So if men wanted to go out and have a drink, my idea was that they were much better off going in two's.

What I did myself after games in New York was to go back to the apartment Mrs. Stengel and I had in the Essex House. We stayed there a number of years, and Edna got so she enjoyed it more and more. She knew all the management, she knew every bellhop, she knew many of the people that lived in the hotel.

Edna got very much interested in the Yankee players and their wives, and took an interest in the way those families grew. There were very few divorces. It got to where there were about fifty young children, and then probably seventy-five. And this is the way it goes on in most all ball clubs.

25

✂ In this story I've been talking mostly about the men on the teams I played with and managed. But there also were many amazing ballplayers on the teams I competed against.

I'd like now to pick the greatest men that played during my years in baseball. This is beginning in 1912, when I first came up to the big leagues, and on through 1960. You can't get it down to just nine men. It's hard enough to get it down to squads of twenty-five men in each league, which is what I've done here.

These are all players that could be stars with the dead ball or the lively ball. Outside of the pitchers, I've gone in for men that could hit. That's the first thing I've looked for.

I'll begin with the National League. At first base you have to go with Bill Terry and John Mize. Mize was a valuable utility man and pinch hitter for me on the Yankees, but he had his greatest years as a regular in the National League. I'll take Terry as the number one man at the position, though, because he was just as amazing a hitter and a little faster on his feet.

Stengel's all-time all-star squads

(1912-60)

National League		American League	
1b	Bill Terry	1b	Lou Gehrig
	Johnny Mize		George Sisler
2b	Rogers Hornsby	2b	Eddie Collins
	Jackie Robinson		Charley Gehringer
			Napoleon Lajoie
ss	Hans Wagner	ss	Joe Cronin
	Ernie Banks		Luke Appling
	Glen Wright		Phil Rizzuto
3b	Frank Frisch	3b	Buck Weaver
	Pie Traynor		
lf	Stan Musial	lf	Ted Williams
	Zach Wheat		
cf	Willie Mays	cf	Ty Cobb
	Edd Roush		Joe DiMaggio
	Duke Snider		Tris Speaker
rf	Paul Waner	rf	Babe Ruth
			Joe Jackson
c	Gabby Hartnett	c	Mickey Cochrane
	Roy Campanella		Bill Dickey
	Ernie Lombardi		Yogi Berra
p	Grover Alexander	p	Walter Johnson
	Christy Mathewson		Bob Feller
	Carl Hubbell		Lefty Grove
	Dizzy Dean		Ed Walsh
	Warren Spahn		Allie Reynolds
	Ed Reulbach		Vic Raschi
	Dazzy Vance		Chief Bender

At second base it has to be Rogers Hornsby. Just think of a right-handed batter that could hit over .400, which Hornsby did three times. He could murder all kinds of pitching.

Next to him I'd put Jackie Robinson. Robinson may not have been the best double-play man I ever saw at second base, but we're talking about a man that could hit the ball and win games. Robinson was a sensational base runner. He annoyed the pitchers when he was on the bases, and that made it easier for the other hitters.

Another great second baseman was Frank Frisch. But I'd rather have him at third base on this team—he played third quite a bit in his first years on the Giants. Frisch was so fast that he could dive for balls and head them off, and then get up and throw the man out. He really had it all—in the field, on the bases and up at the plate, where he hit both right-handed and left-handed. And he was very aggressive.

My other third baseman would be Pie Traynor. He started out as a shortstop. He was amazing on fielding bunts, and he was tall and could jump up high to cut off what looked like two-base hits. He was a sure hitter.

At shortstop, Hans Wagner was the greatest infielder I ever looked at. He could go to his right, go to his left, go over his head, take a relay, throw you out. He was a brilliant base runner, and a base stealer at any time. He was a big man and a terrific hitter.

My second shortstop is Ernie Banks. I'm picking him mostly because of his hitting—he can bother any pitcher —but he also became a good fielder. And after him I'd take Glenn Wright. When Wright was teamed up with Pie Traynor at Pittsburgh, they gave that club a tremendous left side of the infield. And both of them could hit.

In left field, how in the world are you going to get away from Stan Musial? He is going to do something at the plate against almost any style of pitching. And then there was Zach Wheat, who played left field for Brooklyn for so many years. He was the most graceful left-handed hitter I ever saw. With the dead ball, many of his line drives were caught, but they were just shot out of a cannon almost every time up.

In center field, there's no question in my mind that Willie Mays could have played in the olden days. He's an amazing hitter and base runner, and if he can field the way he does with the lively ball, what could he have done with the dead ball, which didn't go so fast in the outfield? He'd catch everything in sight.

The next man in center field would be Edd Roush. He was a great player with the dead ball, and played very good when the lively ball came in. He could hit the ball, he could go and catch it. Then I'd have to go to Duke Snider up to the time he got knee trouble. He was a good catcher of a fly ball. He could throw the ball and hit it for distance.

My right fielder is Paul Waner. For a little man, he was the greatest hitter I ever saw—I didn't see Willie Keeler play. Waner could hit the ball to all fields, and he was a good little fielder in the outfield.

In the catching department I'll have to give it to Gabby Hartnett. He was an amazing thrower, he was a big man, he could hit the home runs. And I'm going for the hitters, which eliminates a catcher like Al Lopez, who was an outstanding man behind the plate.

Campanella is number two. He was a good man back of

the bat and could murder you as a hitter—he had to be brushed back a lot. My third choice would be another big man, Ernie Lombardi. He had a good arm and could hit the ball on the nose—he led the league in batting twice.

Among the National League pitchers I'll start with Grover Alexander. He pitched sixteen shutouts in 1916. He could pitch side arm, he could pitch two-thirds over-handed. Every ball that he threw would break—even his fast ball. Alexander had wonderful control and could pitch to your weaknesses.

Christy Mathewson was another of the greatest pitchers I ever saw. He was the first man I know of to come up with a screw ball—they called it a fadeaway then. Then you have to go to a later pitcher on the Giants that had a won-derful screw ball—Carl Hubbell. And Mr. Hubbell had a terrific disposition for a pitcher. If his club made errors behind him, he wouldn't let it upset him. And he was the kind of a pitcher that could get the big hitters out.

The next man is Dizzy Dean. His career was shortened because he hurt his leg in an All Star Game, but up to then he was amazing. He had a curve ball, a fast ball that jumped, and great control.

Then I come to Warren Spahn. In 1961 he became the thirteenth pitcher in big-league history to win three hundred or more games. Back when I was managing the Boston Braves I saw a little of Spahn before he went into the service in the second World War. He's a left-hander like Whitey Ford, except that he's a bigger man. He can hold runners on first. Then they don't often go from first to third on you, and you get more forceouts at second and more double plays.

Another of the outstanding National League pitchers

was Ed Reulbach back before the First World War. He was a man that could win—he won 182 games and lost only 106.

My last pitcher is Dazzy Vance. He didn't become great until he was over thirty, and then for about ten years he really blasted the ball in there.

That makes seven pitchers, and with a team like this, seven should be enough. In fact, it doesn't seem possible that anybody could beat this club—until you move over to the American League and see what they've got there.

Look what they had at first base. Lou Gehrig was such a terrific hitter they sometimes wondered if he wasn't as good as Ruth, or better than Ruth. The biggest competition for Gehrig was Sisler. He could do almost everything. He ws a .400 hitter twice, and had a lifetime average of .340.

At second base it's Eddie Collins. He could field, he could run bases, he could steal signs. He could hit any kind of pitching, he could place the ball anywhere you wanted it.

My next second baseman is Gehringer. He may not have been as good as some men at double plays, but he was perfection at everything else. He held his bat level, and it looked like when you pitched the ball to him, it struck the bat.

And then you have to take Napoleon Lajoie. I saw him a few times near the end of his career, and I want to tell you, he could still hit that ball. He was a very graceful six-foot man who could cover good ground playing second base.

Now when you go to shortstop, I want the man that could hit the ball farthest, so I'll take Joe Cronin. I think he was the league's best shortstop that could hit the ball hard. And the second good shortstop that could hit was Luke Appling.

As the third shortstop, it's just about a tossup between Aparicio and Rizzuto. Both could do everything except slug the ball. I'm choosing Rizzuto because he possibly was a little better hitter.

At third base I have to pick Buck Weaver. He was put out of baseball in the Chicago Black Sox scandal of 1919, but for ability, he was the best third baseman they had in the American League. He could hit, he could go to his right, he could go to his left. And he had speed.

There have been many fine left fielders in that league, but you have to give the job to Ted Williams. He was the greatest perfectionist I ever saw. Being a left-handed hitter, his park up in Boston was not built for him, just like Yankee Stadium was not built for DiMaggio hitting right-handed. But look how Williams hit, and think what he might have done playing half his games in a home park that was suited for him.

In center field I'll start out with possibly the greatest ballplayer there ever was for being sensational—Ty Cobb. He hit .400 three times. His lifetime average for twenty-four years was .367. He was on the bases all the time, and could beat a ball club all by himself with his stealing and base-running.

Ty died in 1961. He was a good friend of mine. I got some very nice encouragement and suggestions from him while I was managing the Yankees. After we won our fourth straight in 1952 he wrote me, "You should, Casey Stengel, be in Baseball's Hall of Fame. Just remember, I predict this, old boy."

In center field you also have to have Joe DiMaggio,

and then Tris Speaker. I watched Speaker play with the dead ball—he later played with the lively ball too—and he could really catch up with the baseball. He could come in and charge a ground ball better than any outfielder in baseball, and had a great arm. And he was a .344 hitter over a long career.

When you get to right field, there's only one Babe Ruth. And I also have to put there Joe Jackson, who got thrown out in the Black Sox scandal along with Buck Weaver and several others. Jackson had tremendous ability and was a terrific hitter.

There have been some tremendous catchers in the American League. You've got Mickey Cochrane, you've got Bill Dickey and Yogi Berra. They're possibly the three best catchers that have ever been in baseball—better than any in the National League. All three could hit that ball, hit it in the pinch, catch it and throw you out.

Now when you get to pitching, Walter Johnson has to be it. He played mostly with a second-division team but was a big winner anyhow. He had wonderful control and threw bullets.

Bob Feller was probably just as fast. For a number of years he could get anybody out. Then you've got to go to Lefty Grove, an amazing left-handed pitcher that won three hundred games. And Ed Walsh was another great one—a spitball pitcher. He could start every third and fourth day and go nine innings—one year he won forty games.

For the fifth and sixth pitchers, what's wrong with two of my Yankee stars—Allie Reynolds and Vic Raschi? I've told you before how hard they could throw and how good they were.

There were a number of other great pitchers in the

American League, but for my seventh man I'll take Chief Bender. He did an amazing job for Connie Mack's Athletics during the first part of the century.

And there you have my all-stars—twenty-five men from each league. And there'll never be a ball club that has twenty-five men as great as that as long as baseball lives.

26

✂ What did I do with myself after I left
the Yankees at the end of 1960? Well, to start with, Mrs.
Stengel and I have always had a wonderful home life out
in Glendale, California. We've been living in the same
house since we were married in 1924. It's on a lot
about a hundred feet by four hundred feet, with flower
gardens and fruit trees out back, and a tennis court and a
swimming pool. The swimming pool was one of the first
ever built at a private home in Glendale, and it's held up
through earthquakes and everything else.

As I mentioned a while back, we've taken a special interest in seeing Edna's nieces and nephews grow up, not
having children ourselves. On family get-togethers over
the weekends we'd put those kids to play in the tennis
court, which is completely enclosed by a high metal fence.
Now a new generation is coming along, and the family is
still very close.

I've never done any regular off-season work, because let
me tell you, being a baseball manager is pretty close to a
year-round job. The season runs into October, and then
you have the winter baseball meetings in December. On
the Yankees I'd have my instructional school starting in

February. Then came the regular spring training, after which you'd go into another baseball season.

In 1957 my brother-in-law, Jack Lawson, organized the Valley National Bank in Glendale. I became a stockholder and a director, with the idea that I might spend more time with the bank later on. In 1961 we opened a new branch in Toluca Lake, and then we had a merger with four state banks in the area.

So now the Valley National has six units. I have a nice office in the Toluca Lake branch. I'm a vice-president, although I'm still not what you'd call a full-time banker. I tell people my job is to stand in front of the vaults.

Then I went in with several other people on a new golf driving range on National Broadcasting Company property in Burbank. We opened it in the summer of 1961. And I took part in a number of Little League events during the season. My nephew, Casey Mollett, was in one of the leagues.

And I also put in a lot of time on this story. So the way things went, Edna and I weren't able to take any long trips during the year after I left the Yankees, which we thought we might do when I was out of baseball.

Two or three days after I got home there in October of 1960, my phone started ringing with different propositions, and it kept on like that. I turned down offers to go on the stage and in the movies. I also turned down an opportunity to be on television during the baseball season, but I did make guest appearances on a couple of TV programs.

And I had many opportunities to go back in baseball. I don't mean to embarrass any of the capable men that later took the jobs. But I had some amazing offers. Some of them involved more than just managing. I was to get a piece of the ball club, and possibly a piece of an outside business, and perhaps end up making more money than I ever did before.

Actually the baseball propositions started even before I left the Yankees. During the 1960 season a group that hoped to acquire the ownership of the Kansas City club —but didn't succeed in getting it—asked if I'd be interested in going in with them. Then I was approached about the new Continental League that Branch Rickey was trying to start, which included a club in New York City.

Now I'd had some arguments with Mr. Rickey on occasion, but if you think he wasn't an astute, bright, brilliant man in baseball—well, you just don't know what you're talking about. And with the friction that was developing in the Yankee organization, I might have been interested if the Continental League had been ready to start playing in 1961.

As it turned out, the new league fell through, with some of its franchises being taken over by the present major leagues. One of them, naturally, is the New York Mets, who made me their manager.

But that's getting ahead of the story. There were numerous other propositions after the Yankees let me go. Mr. Veeck of the White Sox—who had to sell out his holdings in 1961 because of his health—was interested in hiring me in some capacity. Mr. Fetzer of Detroit and two of the men from his office, Mr. Ferrell and Mr. Campbell, talked to me about coming there.

Then Charles Finley said he was out to buy a ball club and wanted to have me with him. I thought it would be the new Los Angeles Angels, but he got Kansas City instead. Later I heard from the people who did get the

Angels—Mr. Autry and Mr. Reynolds and Mr. Firestone. And I also was sounded out about the new American League franchise in Washington.

I was tempted several times. But all these people wanted to get somebody as soon as possible, and I wasn't ready to commit myself to a new baseball job just then. I finally decided I'd sit out a season and then see how I felt about it. But I'm very grateful to every ball club and official that gave me a chance to get right back in the business.

I saw a number of games out in Los Angeles during my year off. Mr. O'Malley of the Dodgers and Mr. Reynolds and Mr. Autry of the Angels made my summer very pleasant as far as baseball was concerned, because I could go to either park and witness ball games in their company. Many days I took advantage of this.

On several occasions I had George Weiss with me. He had been appointed president of the New York Mets, and was getting things organized for them to start playing in the National League in 1962. He wanted to familiarize himself with the players and owners around the league, and he made three trips to Los Angeles. Each time he talked to me about becoming the manager of the Mets.

When we were seen together at Dodger games in the Los Angeles Coliseum, many of the newspapermen and broadcasters immediately thought that I had already been signed up by Mr. Weiss. But the truth of the fact was that I had not agreed to take any position.

About the twentieth of September, Mr. Weiss began calling me on the phone almost every day. He said he had to have a new manager before the draft meeting at the end of the season, when the Mets and the Houston

Colts would select players from the other National
League teams.

I kept saying he'd better get somebody else, as I didn't
think I wanted to start all over again managing a brand-
new team at my age. But he had the idea that I was the
best man for the job, because he knew I could handle the
playing end of things to his satisfaction, and leave him
free to concentrate on the office end, where there was so
much to be done.

Finally I began to feel that if Mr. Weiss wanted me
that much, maybe I owed it to him, after his many years
of getting me good ballplayers on the Yankees. So on
September 28, I said perhaps I'd accept, after all. He told
me he'd announce it at ten o'clock the next morning.

Later on that day I began to change my mind again.
I was going to call him back and tell him so. But before
I could do it he had some of his owners on the Mets
talk to me.

He put Mrs. Joan Payson on the phone, and she said,
"My goodness, we're enthused about having you come
here, and we're honestly ready to go to considerable ex-
pense to build up the club." Then Don Grant came on, and
he told me the same thing.

Mrs. Payson is a member of the Whitney family. Mr.
Grant is a stockbroker. They also had people in their
group like G. H. Walker, Jr., and Dwight Davis, Jr. And I
said to myself, "Well, these are nice people to work
for." And good owners are very important in baseball.

So all these things influenced me to come back at the
age of seventy-two. A lot of people thought I was wrong.
I'd gone out of baseball with a pretty good record, and
they thought I should stand on it. But I believe that

baseball is larger than Casey Stengel's record. I couldn't turn down this group that is sincerely out to give New York City another fine major-league ball club. I know that this big city needs more than just the one team, for the benefit of the people that live there and for the many visitors that come to town.

I am not starting in again to have another long career as a manager. I only hope that I can help Mr. Weiss build up the club rapidly, because it's not interesting to go five or ten years before you hit the first division. I think Mr. Weiss is one man who might be able to get the job done faster.

I signed with the Mets for very nearly the salary I had with the Yankees. I possibly could have asked for more. But they're having to put out vast sums to get ball-players and set up an organization and also to repair the Polo Grounds, where we have to play until the new city stadium is ready for us. So I didn't think I should add to their costs by demanding $150,000, or something of that sort. I'm thankful to them for wanting me as manager.

There are so many people I'm thankful to in baseball —the different owners I've worked for, the business managers, the league presidents and the other high officials of the game. I had arguments with some of them at times, but it never lasted over a year or so.

Mr. Frick, the commissioner of baseball, has been very good to me. So has Mr. Cronin, the American League president, and now Mr. Giles in the National League. And another wonderful man is Mr. Yawkey, the Boston owner. I know that Mr. Yawkey has done everything he possibly could to advance the game.

Another man I admire is Walter O'Malley, regardless of the criticism he's had. He did a big job in bringing big-league baseball out to Los Angeles and getting his Chavez Ravine stadium started. And when it comes to rebuilding his ball club, he has left some of the other owners far behind the last two or three years.

I've enjoyed the friends I've made among the fans— the ones that are bankers and the ones that are cab drivers. The public has been very good to me. And I appreciate the fact that I was able to work for the Yankees —I know that's what gave me my biggest reputation.

I'm also proud of the other teams I managed that gave their best for me, whether they won or not. I'm proud of the instructional school I started on the Yankees, which has been copied by numerous other clubs. And I'm proud of my platoon system, no matter what some people think of it.

Don't kid yourself that platooning stopped when I left baseball in 1961. Take the two top teams in the National League. In Cincinnati, which won the pennant, Fred Hutchinson kept platooning his infield and his outfield during the year. On the Dodgers, some people criticized Walter Alston for platooning too much. I didn't think he platooned too much. I thought his pitching went bad, and he didn't get the runs-batted-in from his big hitters. It was like on the Yankees when we had our bad year in 1959.

The Yankees in 1961 may not have changed players as much as I had to in certain years, but I noticed that they platooned four different men in left field. The infielders, with more experience, made the pitching look better. Richardson and Kubek became a great combination around second base. Still, Kubek could play other positions. One thing I might have done was to try for a stronger hitter at third base and switch Boyer back to shortstop, where he'd be just as great a fielder as he is at third.

But that's not my business any more. The club I'm concerned with now is the New York Mets. I have a one-year contract. I was offered a contract for two years, but I want to be free to leave if my health should go bad, or anything like that. If it ever gets to where I'm going to handicap this new machine, I'll be the first to know it, and I'll step out of the picture. I found out during my year off that I don't have to have a baseball job to keep from going frantic or nutty.

But it's a great game. I still feel the same way I did when I was asked to go down to Washington to testify before Senator Kefauver's committee, which was investigating professional sports. I'd just finished managing the American League team in the 1958 All Star Game in Baltimore. I hadn't given too much thought to what I'd tell the committee, because I was very much interested in that game, in which the Baltimore people booed the life out of me for putting Berra in to bat for their catcher, Gus Triandos.

When I got up before that committee the next day, I evidently went into more aspects of the baseball business than they'd expected, because there was considerable comment about it afterward. But what I said just came down to this. They wanted to know what I thought of baseball. I told them I was satisfied with it, or else I'd long ago have become a dentist.